Best of the East,
Best of the West

Best of the East, Best of the West

Naren Tambe

Ivy House
Publishing Group
Publishing Group

www.ivyhousebooks.com

PUBLISHED BY IVY HOUSE PUBLISHING GROUP
5122 Bur Oak Circle, Raleigh, NC 27612
United States of America
919-782-0281
www.ivyhousebooks.com

ISBN: 1-57197-358-3
Library of Congress Control Number: 2002114520

Printed in the United States of America

This book is dedicated to my grandmother who couldn't read or write. But she taught me humane values and gave me my first lessons in ecology before the word became popular in the western world.

Thank you, Grandma, for teaching this "educated bump" the duties in life and exposing him to the beauties in nature. You were a great teacher. I wish there were more "uneducated" teachers like you in this insensitive world.

Preface

This is a collection of my scattered thoughts on people, values, and education.

I was born and raised in India. I got my high school and college education there. In 1961 I came to Madison, Wisconsin, to work on doctorate in educational administration and was seriously planning to go back to India after finishing my education. But then I fell in love with the American way of life. I became a citizen. Now, I go to India every year to compare notes. But I prefer to live in the United States.

It was not the money that attracted me to this country. Far from it. Money has certainly helped me buy plenty of books and subscribe to magazines that I could not get in India. I remember very well one incident. I had to go four miles on my bicycle to a doctor's house to get an old issue of *Time* magazine. His German wife, after keeping me waiting for fifteen to twenty minutes, would tell me that her husband had not yet finished reading it! Now here in America, I have the luxury of subscribing to *Time* and *U.S. News and World Report* and several other magazines and throw them away after reading. I have enjoyed this kind of intellectual freedom in addition to other domestic comforts.

However, some of the aspects of the American way of life have not only upset me but have thoroughly enraged me. One such item is America's love affair with guns accompanied by death of innocent children and senseless destruction of property. I understand that the United States was born in violence, but why should it continue to live in violence after two centuries? The idea that guns alone can keep us free and secure is preposterous. In a nuclear age, guns and machine guns don't count! Our emphasis on guns has changed our humane values. We have to reexamine our values. I am mainly worried about American children.

In this collection of essays, there has been constant references made to great leaders and examples given from my relatives, Indian epics and Indian history, as well as leaders like Mahatma Gandhi and King Ashoka. I have tried to learn from great American leaders like Jimmy Carter and spiritual leaders like Baba Ram Dass (alias Richard Alpert), and of course, Dr. Martin Luther King Jr. and Rosa Parks. Their dedication and contribution to the growth of human life has profoundly impressed me as value models. I sincerely hope our young people here and in India will follow their examples.

In the area of values, I have included an essay entitled "Knowing and Doing It." It underscores the tragedy of human beings. We know too well what is good for us, but we do not have the commitment to implement values in our lives. It's a human tragedy because someone might give you good advice, like Duryodhan received from his relative, or set up an excellent example, as Jimmy Carter has, but you have to take that advice into account and act on it. Only about one in a billion does it. We see, we aim, but we never shoot!

I had given this book the title *You Alone Make the Difference* but then changed it to *Best of the East, Best of the West* to make the book appealing to the people in the East and the West. I have learned from the wise men of India and America. My life has been enriched by them.

Our lives are flooded with all sorts of values. We get our values from our relatives, teachers, leaders and our close friends. But we alone make the difference in shaping and molding our lives. We set values and get advice from people, but we lack the commitment to make that difference. It is up to us to change our lives.

Can we make the difference in our lives? Yes, indeed. Please read the essay, "There Is Always a Second Chance in Life." It's my own favorite. King Ashoka, who was a butcher in the first part of his life, later became an harbinger of peace and love. He totally changed his life. On the contrary, Aurangzeb, the Mogul ruler of India in the seventeenth century, was cruel to his Hindu subjects all his life. Even on his deathbed he didn't repent, nor did he ask for forgiveness. He did not avail himself of the second chance in life.

I have dedicated this book to my grandmother, who couldn't read and write but really educated me and showed the beauty and duty in life. I had schooling, but she had education. Her influence on my life is profound and unforgettable. As pointed out in my essay on her, she was really a fountainhead of values. Other teachers, leaders, and some saints have also touched my life. I am grateful to all of them.

I have not written this book to make money but to share my views and values with my readers, mainly with American people. If I can touch one life and make a difference, I will consider myself fully rewarded.

August 2002

Acknowledgments

No literary work is the achievement of one person. It is always a cooperative effort. This book is no exception.

This book was in progress for more than eight years. I wrote and revised my essays several times. Some of my friends made good suggestions regarding the deletion and language of the book. I want to thank all my friends and my relatives for their interest in my book and for their suggestions.

I also take this opportunity to acknowledge my debt to Janet M. Evans, President and Publisher of Ivy House Publishing Group, and the members of her staff for their cooperation and suggestions regarding the printing and presentation of the book.

I owe a deep debt of gratitude to all the great men and my relatives mentioned in the book. I learned from them. They have influenced my life and molded my thinking. I was lucky to be associated and related to some of them.

My Grandmother:
The Foundation of Good Values

God has a peculiar way of compensating human beings. He takes something from us with one hand and replaces it with something else, sometimes something better. I lost my mother when I was seven years old. I don't remember much about her except that she gave me a good thrashing when I broke my friend's slate at school and lied about it. She was trying to teach me something, which I understood later in life. I have been passing on my mother's message to my students for many years. It is very important for human beings to respect the property of others. As a child, I had violated that right, and her thrashing was a reminder of it. But as a teacher, I often ask myself, "Why did she thrash me to give the message?" She could have talked to me and explained the rationale behind thrashing and where I had gone wrong. She could have given me a warning ticket. I guess she was old-fashioned and those were different times. Spanking was so common that many thought it was the only way to discipline your child. Could I have remembered the message if my mother had not spanked me? I don't know.

When my mother died, my father was hardly thirty-eight years old. He never remarried. When I was in college, I asked him the reason about his decision to remain single. He told me he had decided not to remarry because he was not sure about the prospective wife's treatment toward us. In short, he had sacrificed his personal life and pleasure for us. I was profoundly impressed by his noble gesture.

Because there was no woman at home, I spent most of the time at my grandparents' house. Both loved me. They were both religious and practiced what they preached. My grandfather was a strict disciplinarian, but my grandmother, like most grandmothers, was very liberal. She gave me love and protected me when grandfather threatened to spank me. But she did insist on me going to school on time and doing my homework and making good grades. She couldn't read or write but was very much concerned with my education. I was going to be the first high school graduate from my family, and I was determined to make my grandma proud of me. My grandfather had promised me a bicycle on my graduation. Unfortunately neither of my grandparents lived long enough to see me not only graduate from a high school but also earn two bachelor's degrees, three master's degrees, and a doctorate from universities in India and the United States. If my grandparents in India were alive today, I am sure they would have given me a brand-new Mercedes Benz as a graduation gift!

There were a few occasions when I did not agree with my grandma at all. I thought she was crazy. Since she didn't have education, her decisions sometimes were not based on reason. She had her own fads and superstitions.

India is a poor country, and we have a bumper crop of beggars on streets and at railway stations. In my opinion, they are a nuisance to the society. Some of them were lazy and did not want to work for a living. People give them food at homes and in front of temples. My grandma was no exception. She invariably gave food to any beggar who came to her house at noon.

She told me that at noon, God comes to our house in the form of a beggar, and we should never turn away anyone.

Many beggars played on the religious and the superstitious side of the old people. These beggars selected homes with great care. They knew how to appeal to the religious side of old people like my grandmother. I could see their game clearly but was unable to convince my grandmother that those beggars were selfish and loafers. They wanted a free lunch and didn't want to work for their food.

My grandma would not listen to my intellectual mumbo-jumbo and would always ask me to keep quiet and feed the poor beggars. I have believed in the philosophy of self-help and a strong work ethic. Free food and handouts degrade many human beings. One should work, if one is strong and healthy, for one's living. When I worked in our city's soup kitchen program, I had my differences with the director on this question. I thought they were carrying on my grandmother's old tradition. Feed all and ask no questions! I noticed that at least half of our clients in the soup kitchen were strong and healthy enough to work for their living. Some even helped us in the preparation and distribution of food. But many came to eat because the food was free! I thought it was very degrading to them and affected their self-esteem. When I offered one person to help me in my garden at $6 an hour, he was mad at me. I never forgot the look on his face. He thought I had insulted him by asking him to earn his bread!

My grandmother loved not only beggars but also birds, animals, and plants. Every morning she worshiped the *tulsi* (basil, a sacred plant in India) plant and made seven rounds around it, asking for its blessings. I used to laugh at her irrational behavior. She knew I didn't share her views on plants, birds, and animals. She would try to convince me. "Naren, there is a universal soul in all of us. We are a part of the total universe. Learn to respect all birds, animals, beasts, trees, and plants. They have souls, too." She really practiced what she preached. Before I ate my food in the morning, I had strict instructions to serve a full dish and take it out the house to feed cows and crows. Sometimes those hungry creatures would give me a bad time by pushing me aside, and crows would sit on my tiny head. Again, I said to myself that this crazy woman cared more for birds and animals than for me. I had to respect and feed the animals even though they handled me roughly!

I often asked myself: "Doesn't this old woman understand that I, too, was hungry and was getting late for the school?" I used to murmur: *dumb animals and dumb grandma!* On the way back to kitchen, I had to clean my hands before I touched my food. She always reminded me to say the famous prayer with folded hands in Sanskrit from the *Upanishads,* "Oh Lord, let all the people of the world be happy. Let there be peace. Let there be peace in the universe."

For many years I taught a course in human relations. But I used to substitute human relations with universal relations. The term *universal relations* is much more comprehensive and includes all human beings plus birds, animals, trees, and plants. In short, it has ecology built in it.

As I look back, I wonder who inspired me to think this way. I had no doubt that it was the influence of my "crazy" grandmother who couldn't read and write but had taught me to love and respect the animate and inanimate objects in life. How important it is for us to learn and practice this lesson! I learned from books, and my grandmother learned from life. I merely had schooling, but she had real education. I was an educated bump, and she was a great teacher. What a difference!

Thank you, Grandma, for coming into my life and teaching me good values.

IT HAPPENED ON FATHER'S DAY

Sometimes teachers read a story and discuss it in the class. We understand the words contained in the story, but seldom do we grasp its depth and the underlying meaning the writer is trying to convey. I had to come all the way to the United States to understand the true meaning of the story I had taught to my high school students in India.

The story is written by India's Nobel Prize–winning poet Rabindranath Tagore.* The title of the story is "Cabuliwalla." This famous story is included practically in every Indian textbook. I read the story in my seventh-grade class in India. Neither my teacher nor I was interested in the story, which is based on the life of a traveling salesman—a Pathan—who comes to Calcutta to sell dry fruit to make a living. I strongly felt that the story was included in the textbook simply because its author had won the Noble Prize for literature in 1913. His close friendship with Mahatma Gandhi must have influenced the decision of the textbook committee. I saw no merit in the story as a reader. I also thought that story was not very exciting.

The vendor—Cabuliwalla—visits the city of Calcutta once a month to sell the dry fruits from Afghanistan, and he stops by the narrator's house to sell his stuff. The narrator has an eight-year-old daughter named Mini. Every time

Cabuliwalla visits the narrator's home, he makes it point to say "hello" to Mini and finds time to play with her. There is nothing common between the two. He hardly speaks her language. He is a middle-aged man, and a Muslim by religion; Mini is a young Hindu girl. He tried to win her friendship by giving her dry fruits, which she dearly loves. Their friendship grows slowly. They talk and laugh. Mini's mother, a conservative Hindu, is very suspicious about their growing friendship. In her heart, she does not like the tall, well-built Muslim vendor. She warns her husband against the man who was getting closer to her daughter. The narrator is too busy with his work and sees no harm in their innocent friendship. He ignores her warnings.

According to the prevailing Indian custom, Mini was to be given away in marriage soon. One day when the vendor comes to their home to sell dry fruit, he hears the auspicious music being played—Mini was being groomed for the marriage ceremony. Cabuliwalla is upset at this. He understands that it is a wedding day, and indeed a happy occasion for Mini. It is hard for him to part company with his little friend, because he was not going to see her in future. He is very sad and upset. He meets her father and begs him to allow him to see Mini for the last time. Mini's mother is set against it. She will not allow any Muslim person to see her Hindu daughter on her wedding day. It was unthinkable for her. Cabuliwalla explains why he was dying to see Mini for the last time. To convince Mini's father, he brings out a paper from his pocket that carries a print of a palm. He shows the paper with the palm print to the author and tells him, "Sir, I do not have a picture of my daughter to show you, but believe me this is print of my daughter's palm. I have always carried it in my pocket wherever I go. Your daughter, Mini, always reminds me of my own daughter who is thousands of miles away from me. Please allow me to see her one more time. I want to wish her all the best." Being a father himself, the narrator is touched by his explanation and, over the protestation of his wife, allows him to see Mini for the last time.

With tears in his eyes, Cabuliwalla looks at Mini from a distance and wishes her all the best on the auspicious occasion. The narrator gives the vendor some money to cover his travel expenses. The vendor believes that his reunion with his daughter, even if she is living in a far-off place like Kabul, Afghanistan, will bring happiness to his daughter.

This is a simple story. As a student and a teacher I thought it was unrealistic. Only later did I realize painfully that I did not have experience to really appreciate the depth and experience of the narrator. A visit to America provided me that opportunity and gave me the insight about the universal bond that existed between Mini and the Cabuliwalla as well as the narrator and the vendor who came to his house not only to sell dry fruits but for something else too.

I came to the United States for higher education in 1961 and studied in Madison, Wisconsin, for a year. Like all other foreign students, I also experienced a cultural shock. Away from my family and the culture of my country, everything was new to me. The people, the language, and their customs. Even as an adult, I had a hard time adjusting to the new situation.

One evening I visited a huge store in downtown Madison. It was a four-story department store. I was impressed by its management style. Americans like to do everything on a large scale and, if successful, they like to open chain stores to expand their business. It was one such chain store. I was having a good time looking (to be exact, window shopping!) at items for sale. I was about to buy some candy when I observed a little boy with golden hair looking at candies behind the glass walls with a watery mouth. I sensed his purpose and asked him to point out what type of candy he wanted. Meanwhile he told me his name was Robin. I bought the candy of his liking, and I felt very good inside. My joy didn't last long. Robin's mother came looking for him. Having found him with handful of candy, she inquired how he got the candy. I politely told the lady that I had bought it for her son, Robin. Instead of thanking me for the candy, she remarked, "You know you should not give candy to children since it is not good for their teeth. Robin, please return the candy to the gentleman." I never expected such a reaction to my "sweet" gesture. I was terribly disappointed. She handed over the box of candy and was about to leave. I begged her to stop. I told her that Robin—her son—reminded me of my only son, who was 13,000 miles away in India. To convince her I showed the picture of my son to her. She looked at it and seemed to have changed her stiff attitude, "I am sorry. I understand your feelings now. Okay, Robby, take the candy and let's go home. Did you thank the gentleman?" I put my hand on Robin's head and said, "You don't have to thank me. It's okay."

I came out of the department store with tremendous satisfaction. Robin made me home-sick. I longed to meet my seven-year-old son in India. If I had wings to fly, I would have taken off then and there. How I wished he were with me! I took out his picture from my wallet and looked at it closely. How he had whistled loudly when my steamer took off from Bombay harbor!

Then all of a sudden, I thought of Tagore's story of Cabuliwalla. I realized from my own experience what the famous author was trying to communicate to his readers. It was a story of a father, by a father, and for a father like me to enjoy! Didn't I act like a Cabuliwalla in an American department store? The poor vendor who came to Calcutta didn't even have the picture of his daughter to show the narrator. So he showed the print of her palm to convince him. I showed the American lady the picture of my son. I was no different as a Hindu father from the Muslim father Cabuliwalla. The narrator from Calcutta, the vendor from Kabul, and I were all bound by a universal fatherly feeling.

When I was a student and teacher, I couldn't understand the story, much less enjoy it because I was not a father at the time. My new role as a father and separation from my son for many months made Tagore's story at once lively and personal.

Now I know why Tagore was such a great writer. I read Cabuliwalla as a student, taught the story as a teacher but, more important, I understood and enjoyed it the most as a father.

Notes

* On Rabindranath Tagore

1. Tagore, Rabindranath, *The Home and the World.* (Video recording by National Film Development Corporation of India. Los Angeles: Embassy Home Entertainment, 1986.)

2. Tagore, Rabindranath, *Sacrifice and Other Plays.* Delhi: Macmillan Company of India, 1980.

3. Tagore, Rabindranath (ed.), *The Collected Poems and Plays of Rabindranath Tagore.*

4. Tagore, Rabindranath, "Cabuliwalla." Edited by Gujarat Government, Textbook Committee, 1993.

THE EXCEPTIONAL TEACHER

I have had very unpleasant experiences as a student in India. The classroom punishment and spanking were so common and routine that parents and students looked on them as a necessary part of learning. That was the price you paid for learning. No student dared to complain to his parents lest he be beaten at home again! Parents did not entertain any complaints against teachers. They believed teachers more often than their own kids. Parents thought that the teachers were all good guys and the students were little devils who needed to be disciplined.

The king of our princely state was an education-minded king. He had introduced compulsory free education and had started mobile libraries for students and teachers as far back as 1891. The books were delivered to us in our neighborhood in wooden boxes. He encouraged democracy in his state and awarded scholarships to poor and deserving students. One such student (an untouchable) later on went to the London School of Economics and Columbia University in New York and became the law minister of India. He drafted the constitution of India. Surprisingly, this royal king of my state did not have even high school education!

In India I lived in front of an elementary school. I used to look at the three-story beautiful building, which the king had built to promote elementary education. But I also wondered why every morning many parents had to beat their children and had to drag them to that beautiful school. *Why are the children afraid of schools?* I asked myself. Are these schools or prisons? One day, when I went inside the school, the story started unfolding. I heard the children crying when they were spanked and beaten heavily. One teacher threw a student's head against the wall. I saw many students standing outside their classrooms as a part of their punishment. They were all talking with one another while the teacher was teaching their friends inside.

When I came home I thought I had just visited the Bastille. How could children learn under these conditions? No wonder they were crying when they were being dragged to school. Schools to them were slaughterhouses where they were being offered as sacrificial lambs! In some cases, for minor offenses teachers humiliated their students by hanging a slate around his neck with words written on it: "I am a thief. I stole my friend's pencil." It's terribly humiliating. But the teacher was more concerned with the physiology rather than psychology of the student. He didn't gave a damn how students felt about it. How do you expect such students to like and respect their teachers? To many teachers, beating was a means of promoting education. They sincerely believed in the old maxim, "Spare the rod and spoil the child."

No wonder I looked on the schools as prison. The schools and the teachers in charge of education destroyed the love for learning and turned off many students who might have otherwise graduated from a high school.

As I grew older I thought that not teachers alone but the boring school curriculum also turned the place of learning into place of punishment. Even after my own graduation I used to have nightmares about my school. Describing my school experience, I had written a poem. I wrote: "Every time I look at palms / black, brown and red / I cry with joy / I am so glad / that all my teachers are dead."

I had given a full-blown expression to my built-up anger and frustration in my poem. I don't hate any teachers, but I certainly condemn their cruel methods to promote learning. There are others who believe in the efficacy of the rod. If it were true, I would have been a genius!

Having been tortured by teachers and bored by meaningless school curriculum, I lost interest in school. During one summer vacation, I met a gentleman who was a relative of our neighbor. I was introduced to him by his aunt, who lived in our neighborhood. When I was told that he was a teacher in a school near Bombay, I could not believe my ears and eyes. He was so kind and mild in his manners. There was eternal smile on his face. He talked so softly that I thought he used only vowels and avoided harsh consonants to avoid inflicting harm on any one. I also learned that he was a follower of Gandhi and a well-known literary figure who had translated Goethe's *Faust,* Victor Hugo's *Les Miserables,* Jane Austen's *Silas Marner,* and Walt Whitman's *Leaves of Grass,* and well as Charles Dickens's *David Copperfield* and many other Western classics. He had done all these translations for children, whom he loved so much. His famous couplet printed on all his books was "Those who entertain children are nearer to God."

This new teacher I met was totally opposite the ones I had encountered in my school days. He was kind, compassionate, and well read as well as socially and politically active. He struck a chord in my brain and heart. He was the teacher I had been looking for all my life. I wanted him to teach me in the classroom and be around me all the time. He was a hard-to-believe teacher. He had written a novel based on his experience, entitled *My Mother.* *When I read it, I cried. I thought he was talking about *my* mother. It was the best-seller and was printed and reprinted more than sixty times. It has been translated into all major Indian languages. I have also read its English translation. It's a simple and very touching story of his mother, who gave him the stuff of his life. He has written in his book that if there if there is any good in his life, he owed it to his mother. She showed him the beauty and duty in life. I have read this book many times with tears in my eyes because I lost my mother when I was hardly eight years old. What joy he created in the lives of millions of children like me! I loved to read his books and hated to go to my school. Many students like me stayed in school because their parents forced them. It was not a garden, and we were neither flowers nor our teachers gardeners. They were simply butchers.

But this new teacher I met also changed my attitude on education totally. He made me look at the role of parents in education and the importance of love in promoting learning. The new teacher I met was never married. He was a great writer as well as a hypnotic speaker. He used his pen and tongue to rouse the social consciousness of the Indians and fight injustice in society. He earned millions of rupees (an Indian currency) by writing books but gave all his money to charity, especially to his students, who were too poor to buy textbooks or pay their tuition. He loved all children as if they were his own. He was truly exceptional as an individual and teacher.

He fasted unto death to bring about the social changes in the western part of India. There was a very famous temple there, and the trustees would not open it to the untouchables. Because it was a private property, the state or the central government could not do anything about it. The untouchability was abolished in India when the country became independent, but it was still practiced in public. The situation reminds me about the social problem we had in the south in America during the civil rights movement. Gandhi advised the teacher to give up fasting to bring about change of hearts in the trustees. But my teacher would not listen to Gandhi and continued his fast for eighteen days. Finally a compromise was reached, the temple was thrown open to the untouchables, and his life was saved. I prayed for him and when I heard the good news, I was so happy. It was the crowning moment of his life. He had proved his point by resorting to nonviolent means to help solve the age-old problem of caste prejudice in India.

When Mahatma Gandhi was assassinated in 1948, the teacher fasted again to atone for the sins of the people who had systematically spread poison against Gandhi for years. They were dangerous and misguided Indians. He wanted to end his own life because he had seen his idol smashed to pieces right in front of his eyes. What hurt him most was the fact that the assassin came from his own state and spoke the same mother tongue. Gandhi's violent death had shaken the teacher's faith in humanity. He asked, "Will we ever learn?" He knew that the earth was not ready for the saints to walk on it. His poetic heart could not absorb the shock of Gandhi's killing. Finally, on June 12, 1953, he committed suicide by taking sleeping pills. Millions mourned his death, and it was a personal loss to me. He had touched my life without even teaching me in a classroom. Truly he was a remarkable teacher in every sense of the word.

Here was an unforgettable teacher who never taught me in a school but showed me the direction in life. I will never forget him.

Notes

* On P. S. Sane
1. Sane, P. S., "Shyamchi Aai" ("Shyam's Mother"). Pune: Anath Vidhyarathi Griha, 1948.

OUR VALUE-ORIENTED PRESIDENT

It is very difficult to assess the popularity of the U.S. president. When they are in office, they make a lot of political mistakes in domestic or international affairs and often become very unpopular with the American public. As a result, they go down in the popularity rating. But as time goes by and when the dust has settled down, people have another look at their presidents. Some look much better depending on what they do after they leave office. It happened to President Harry Truman and Teddy Roosevelt. Truman succeeded Franklin D. Roosevelt, and he had to make a very crucial decision about bombing Hiroshima and Nagasaki to end World War II. It was arguably the most difficult decision that was ever made by any U.S. president. Truman showed tremendous courage and insight in making that historical decision. He did not care for his popularity, nor did he wait for the polls to dictate his decision. He acted according to the dictates of his conscience and considered the national interest and the larger interest of humanity. History tells us Truman was right. World War II ended after the bombing on Japan.

The presidents who look great as presidents when they are in power may not be judged as great presidents by history. Times change and so do the attitudes of the people.

This is the story of one such president who failed on many political fronts when he was in the White House. He ran for a second term, but the time was out of joint and he lost the presidency. What he did in the post presidency period to promote international understanding and help the poor in the world made him a different leader, and he is now one of the towering leaders of the world. Through his example he showed all of us how we can lead meaningful and productive lives. We may lose some battles here and there, but we can still win a war in life at the end.

This man is Jimmy Carter.

I was never a great fan of President Jimmy Carter when he came to power in 1972. His religious bent sometimes turned me off. But Carter is not a religious hypocrite. He follows and practices the religion so beautifully as defined by William Penn, "to help mend the world." He may not have Kennedy's charisma, nor was he a great communicator like Reagan. But Jimmy Carter has moral character and deep compassion for humanity. As historians now acknowledge, he has high level of intelligence. (Remember: He was once a nuclear physicist, and not just a peanut farmer). Carter had a big problem with the hostage situation in Iran, and it took his toll in his reelection bid for the presidency. But the two highlights of his presidential tenure—the Camp David Accords and the Panama Canal treaties—should not be forgotten.

In my opinion, Carter is the only president who looks taller and better as a human being than as a president. I am sure that his mother, Lillian Carter, and his sincere religious commitment have played a vital part in the development of his moral character. And he has greatly built on it. He has not wasted his time by being on the boards of big American companies, as did Gerald Ford and George Bush Sr. and getting highly paid for doing little work. Nor did he undertake a lecture tour like Reagan and made $1 million a speech!

This president turned his life around by being a spokesman for the poor in the underdeveloped countries in Asia and Africa. He visited the troubled areas and offered to mediate in their disputes, saving lives and money. He also started the Carter Center in Atlanta and invited international dignitaries to discuss and get insight into international problems.

Carter has also written many books to stimulate the thinking of the American people and has motivated them through the humanitarian projects like Habitat for Humanity. With a hammer in his hand, he himself has helped build homes for the poor in America. When the poor have cried, Carter has rushed to wipe their tears. In this respect he seems guided by Buddha's compassion for the poor.

He has also stood beside the common man and has not hesitated to criticize big companies like Weyerhaueser, Georgia -Pacific, and International Paper, who damage our ecology and put small landowners out of business. Carter was a strong supporter of the North American Free Trade Agreement, but he comes down hard on those businesspeople and industrialists who use the process of globalization at the cost of human suffering How many presidents have acted this way to help humanity? Carter has given Christianity a good name. He has shown the world how a good Christian should act, or for that matter how a good human being should act for the benefit of humankind.

Jimmy Carter has been America's great role model for the young and the old to follow. He most assuredly deserved the Nobel Prize for Peace, which he was awarded in 2002.

LATE BLOOMERS IN EDUCATION

Have you observed that some of flowers blossom late but once they start blooming, they do so beautifully? I have noticed the same phenomenon in education. Teachers have a tendency to pass a judgment on some students, especially those who are not doing so well in academic studies, and possibly condemn them as "good for nothing." It's as if we have already given up on them. In India, I made that mistake as a teacher and found out how wrong I was about my own student. As I look back, I feel very bad about it now.

It happened a long time back. I was the youngest principal of a junior/senior high school in my city Baroda (now renamed Vadodara) in India. We loved our students, and they loved us back. We were in good touch with all students' parents. Despite of our best efforts, there were some students whom we couldn't handle satisfactorily. We used all educational techniques to discipline them. Nothing worked. The problem students were disturbing classes and preventing others from learning. Some parents complained frequently and threatened to take their children to another school. Ours was a new school, and we needed children badly to meet our expenses and push our educational and social agenda.

There was one student who was a gang leader and created a king-size headache for me. Many parents and some class students had complained about his rude behavior. Several times I had called the boy's father and warned him about his son's rude behavior in the class. The father apologized to me every time and went home and chided his son with a sermon to behave properly.

It worked for only a week. His son would be back to square one again. All of our teachers were fed up with his behavior. All of us believed that this naughty boy was a major problem. I was asked by our academic board to call his father and ask him to take his son elsewhere. I couldn't understand why he was behaving that way. I called his father and informed him about the decision of the academic board. He started crying in my office for the behavior of his son

"Mr. Tambe, he is my only son. Please give him another chance. Don't kick him out. I will always be grateful to you." I liked the boy, although I couldn't understand his behavior. With special permission of the academic board, I decided to give him a last chance to shape him up before we shipped him out forever.

Shortly afterward, in 1961, I left India. I came to the University of Wisconsin, Madison, to work on doctorate in educational administration. I got a golden opportunity to be in a beautiful setting and forget all about the problem child back home. The headache was gone. I felt relieved. The mental pressure was gone, but that problem-child remained at the back of mind. He wouldn't leave!

After finishing my own education, I went to India for a visit after many years. I was thrilled to visit India after such a long time, but I became sick with dysentery. My stomach was upset, and I had to go to bathroom several times a day. I decided to go to the nearest doctor in my neighborhood. I was so weak I could hardly walk. As is usually the case in India, there was a long line of patients in my doctor's office, and some were outside his office waiting for him. I thought he must be a very popular, if not a competent, doctor. Like others, I waited for a long time in his waiting room. He came late in his new car.

A well-built young man came greeting his patients on the way to this office. I looked at him and thought I had seen his face somewhere. The doctor immediately recognized and touched my feeble feet to show his respect in the Indian style. "Mr. Tambe, when did you come from America? It seems that you have stayed too long in a foreign land to recognize your former student at your school. I am Deepak Shah."

I felt ashamed to confess that I had failed to recognize my former student who had turned out to be an outstanding and one of the leading doctors in our city. I was so proud and equally shocked to know that he was none other than the one who had been such a headache to me in our school! He was that student whose parent I had to call every week with a request to take him out of our school so that other students in his class could learn. All our techniques of discipline had been unsuccessful in his case. Some of our teachers and parents had strongly advised me to kick the naughty boy out of school permanently. I was so glad that I had not taken their advice.

I gave him warning and one more chance to shape up. It's no guarantee. But it worked in this case. As a result, our city had gained an outstanding and a dedicated doctor.

A week after that, I was invited to his home for dinner. Later I learned that he had started a medical clinic project in rural part of India to help the poor. He also told me that one day a week he examines his very poor patients free of charge. He had passed all medical exams in Malaysia and Canada with honors. My problem student at school had started to solve the medical problems of his patients. I was proud of the fact that, like many other doctors in our city, he was not only interested in making money but was committed to alleviate the suffering of humanity. He was influenced by the work and example of Mahatma Gandhi, Mother Teresa, and Albert

Schweitzer and teachers like me (that's what he told me). The ugly duckling had turned into a beautiful swan! I don't take any credit for his transformation. But as a teacher I am certainly proud to say he was my student. Now I firmly believe that some flowers blossom late, but when they blossom, they do so beautifully.

My conclusion of this story is: *Never* give up on flowers or children! No wonder the German educationist Froebel called his school a kindergarten!

MY CONTENTED FATHER

In the United States, we make too much fuss over a single-parent family and its impact on the family and learning. For many years in India, I didn't fully realize that I was brought up by a single parent. It happened that my mother died when I was hardly seven years old. My father could have married again. He was only thirty-nine when he was widowed. He told me later that he decided not to remarry because he was not sure whether the new woman would take good care of his four children. It was my first glance at father's personal sacrifice for all of us.

To be honest, I don't know what it *is* to have a mother in the house. I had two brothers and one sister. When my mother died, we had to take care of each other. I remember vividly how I fed my baby sister with my hands and dressed her every morning before she went out to play in the neighborhood. We took turns cooking and cleaning up the kitchen. There was no dining table because there was no dining room. We all sat on the floor to eat. We could not touch our food until father started eating first. It was a signal for us to start eating. We followed him to show our respect. There was no electric light. We used old-fashioned lanterns at night. My father used coals every morning to make hot tea for all of us. We didn't miss a thing! We were poor by Indian standards, but we were happy.

We didn't have a radio or a TV, nor did we have any gadgets to entertain us. We went outside and played marbles, cricket, and other Indian games in streets.

Whatever the season, my father got up always at five o'clock in the morning He would prepare hot tea and would try, in vain, to wake us. I was the worst. I was a night reader. I read all night and slept during the morning. I got up late, bathed, ate lunch, and went to school. My father always criticized my way of living. He would often quote, and I could clearly hear in my sleep, "Early to bed and early to rise, makes a man healthy, wealthy, and wise." If it were true, my father would have been a multimillionaire!

He was poor all his life in terms of money. But he was so contented that he put me to shame by showing how we should cut down on our worldly needs. "Naren, learn to be happy with what you have. Don't run after the mirage." My father had only two pairs of pants and only one pair of shoes. He washed one pair and wore it the next day. I was the opposite of my father. I had more than fifteen pairs of pants and more than a dozen shirts. My father would criticize my wardrobe and urge me reduce my wants. I was too young to follow his impractical advice. I thought he was living in another world.

When I came to America, I soon realized that my father was right and I was wrong about buying clothes and shoes I hardly used. The hunger for buying was never satiated. In the beginning, I blamed the capitalist society that used glaring ads to whet our buying needs. I sometimes bought items on sale that I was not going to use for months. Why do I want to buy items today? I was brainwashed into thinking that I was going to save money in the long run. As consumers we are led to believe that we save by spending. Should I still blame the capitalist society? Why did I allow myself to be influenced by the messages from sponsors? It was not the ads but my inability to control my ever increasing appetite for buying that created my financial problems.

My father always taught me to live within my means. When I came to America, I bought items on credit cards. I had excellent credit, and banks were sending me cards every month and increasing my limit so that I could buy more and stay in debt forever! I got into terrible debt, which I couldn't handle. Several times I thought of declaring bankruptcy. But my father had also taught me a good lesson: "If you owe anything to anybody, return it or pay it back. Don't cheat anyone." It was good moral advice he had prescribed for all of his children. My father taught me to respect material wealth but not get trapped into it.

The most important gift he gave was the art of contentment. It was not idle talk. He was a teacher, but he never told us to do as he did, but follow him as he lived. It was a hard lesson for me to practice in a country where citizens are seduced into buying useless items, most of them which we can live without. The surrounding competition and the artificial need of impressing others keep us tied down to never-ending debt. No wonder more than 70 percent of Americans are heavily in debt. We sacrifice our family's future to enjoy present luxuries. To me, this is not an American way of life!

Can I ever follow my father's advice and go to back to his simple way of life and be contented like he was? I knew too well that through the art of contentment, he had earned his inner peace. I am struggling hard to learn that art. I realize too well, like many of us do, that once you ride the tiger, it's very difficult to get off his back.

AT THE FEET OF THE MASTER

Indian culture has always respected the three S's in any human being: scholarship, simplicity, and sacrifice. In an age where now we worship heroes with simple thinking and high living, people who symbolize such noble ideals have become a dying breed. I never thought I would ever come face to face with such a simple and a scholarly saint. To me, he was a saint teacher.

When I met him in India, I was studying philosophy and education in college. I was appointed as a principal of a middle school in a village which was only thirty miles away from my city. The total population of the village was fewer than 400 people, most of them farmers. The place was lonely, but so picturesque! The river that flowed around the village nurtured the basic needs of the people and enhanced its natural beauty. After a long day at school, I would sit down at the bank of the river and listen to distant noises of the villagers. Sometimes all-pervading serenity was shattered by barking dogs. It was so peaceful there that I felt nearness to God. Being a city person all my life, I appreciated the quiet village life more. Every day I ate fresh vegetables, drank fresh milk, breathed fresh air, and heard the cry of the inner voice. How I miss that in America!

I was new to village life at the time. I soon discovered that some our teachers and lots of our students made frequent trips to a nearby village to get the blessings of a holy man. Most of the time they visited him on either Thursdays or Sundays. They told me all sorts of weird stories about this man. Being an Indian myself, I didn't pay much attention to their stories in the beginning because most religious preachers in India are either showmen or fake. They perform all sorts of tricks to make money and mislead the common folks. I was also very active in politics. Naturally, I had developed a built-in hostility toward such religious miracle workers. I never trusted them. But this man's followers at the school told me some unusual stories about him that aroused my curiosity. I decided to pay him a visit if not receive his blessings. Later on, I understood the meaning of Goldsmith's famous lines, "those who came to scoff, remained to pray."

The place where this man lived was four miles from our village. The only mode of communication was going there by a bullock cart or walking on my two feet. I decided to walk with some of teachers and students. It was a new experience for me. My friends at school were making these trips by foot every week. He was called Rang Avadhuta Swami.

We reached there at six o'clock. It being a Sunday, lots of people from the surrounding villages and many from cities had already gathered under a big neem tree to take *darshan* (bowing with respect) of this religious teacher.

I was anxious to take a close look at this guru. The mystery was to be lifted. I must also mention here that stories surrounding this man had started impressing me even though I had my lurking doubts about him. I had gathered more information about this him. He did not speak for the whole week, except Sunday, and he never touched money. He was once a colleague of Mahatma Gandhi and taught at a state university before he decided to renounce the world. This was quite an impressive record. I had read the life of another great Indian spiritual leader—Arbind Ghosh—who spent his life in silence and in seclusion until his death. I decided to keep my mind open in this case.

When the sun was about to rise over the holy river (to an Indian mind, all rivers are holy), he appeared before the devotees with folded hands to greet them. The people got up and, as is the custom, bowed before him to show respect. Some children went near him to offer fruit and flowers (he would not accept money) to show their respect . He accepted fruit and offered blessings to them, but he touched nothing. I was most impressed by his plain clothes. In fact, he was almost naked. He had his underwear and a simple white cloth across his chest. He also used a pair of black glasses to avoid direct sunlight. He walked in his *ashram* (abode) in his wooden sandals. I thought he was at peace with himself. I also noticed he chose his words very carefully before he uttered them. My first impression was very favorable. But I asked myself, *so what?* He is a scholar. I admire a person who has intelligence and selflessness combined. He had passed the first test I had in mind.

After almost an hour, I was introduced to him by one of my staff members who had been his disciple for many years and knew him personally. I was introduced as a new principal in a neighboring village school. He smiled and asked me about my family as well as the school. I told him that I was working on my a master's degree and requested him to help me understand some problems and terms in Indian philosophy. He had a beautiful sense of humor. He laughed at my statement. "Mr. Tambe, you are an unusual person. You have just seen here why people come to me and with what demands. All I have been telling them is to lead a clean life and pray to God daily. I can't solve their family or monetary problems. I don't perform miracles. They don't realize that they create their own problems. But in your case, I will be glad to help you whatever way I can. I am glad your request is not mundane." I asked him when I could come to see him.

He said, "Sharp at five in the morning on next Sunday. And keep your questions ready." "Five in the morning?" It means I had to start walking at three or use a cart to reach the place by five. But I must admit I was thrilled by his presence. I had never seen such a man in my life. I had met thousands of religious bigots and political hypocrites. They come dime a bushel in India. But never a saint who stayed away from money (the root of all evil) and led a silent, spiritual life in a remote village. I was lucky to have met him.

I started meeting him when it was convenient for both of us. Sometimes in a monsoon season it was difficult to walk through mud and rains. Early in the morning, I had difficulty in finding a cart. If I didn't go, he understood. I could not call him in advance to cancel or postpone my appointment because neither of us had phones. In fact, nobody had a phone in the village I lived in! I thought it was a blessing in disguise.

The format of our conversations was simple. I would ask him a question about my problems and difficulties in philosophy. He would then quietly think over the question and elaborate on it for five or ten minutes. When I didn't understand something, I would politely ask him to explain it. It was a question-and-answer session rarely followed by challenges or counterarguments. I could visualize in a small way how Plato must have felt when he learned from Socrates. In ancient India, this was a common mode of learning. The students stayed with their masters for twelve years and learned at their feet.

Most of the time I was a passive listener and an avid absorber. During our many sessions I also learned that he had worked with Mahatma Gandhi for some time when he launched his first *satyagraha* (insistence on truth) movement from the capital of our state, Gujarat.

I loved Socrates, Plato, and Aristotle. I must confess that in the beginning I didn't understand their works completely as a student. I did not have intellectual maturity or life experiences to understand their works. Plato wanted to change society. So did I. I was active in politics for the same reason. I couldn't understand why this great teacher left a great leader like Gandhi and chose to lead a secluded life. When I found the right opportunity, I asked him about it. He knew that I was a radical socialist and a follower of Gandhi. But he had refrained from making any comments about my political activities or party politics. He rarely talked about politics. And I was a political animal. I asked him why he had decided to part company with Gandhi. He said, "First, my inner voice told me that I was not cut out for politics. What was good for Gandhi was not necessarily good for me. Second, Gandhi was a remarkable leader who practiced what he preached. And he was extremely disciplined and dedicated to public welfare. The day-to day hassle in politics was too much for me. I hated politics for its hypocrisy. Politics is a dirty game and it is made dirtier by dirty politicians. Gandhi was a pure twenty-two-carat gold. There was not a bone of selfishness in his body. He was one of the most exemplary leaders of this century. Naren, if you want to change the society, change yourself first. It's the best way to do it. And read what the Eastern and Western philosophers have found after their long search for truth. And remember this: You cannot change this world an iota!" I thought he was giving me a lesson on Gandhi and a Marxist approach to the solution of world problems. What he was telling my restless mind was that I have to heal myself first before I started healing others.

I didn't agree with him then because I was firmly convinced of changing society through capture of political power and using it for the benefit of the poor. The favorite slogan "the greatest good of the greatest number" had more sway over my mind at that time.

As I look back after so many years, I realize the depth and importance of the message of the silent master, more so in this country, where we are brainwashed daily by the electronic and print media. I am also cured of socialism and all economic and political ideologies. We hardly find time to look into ourselves. The master showed me the importance and strength of silence in the spiritual development of human beings. As I pondered over his six days of silence in a week, I realize its importance in getting in touch with our inner self. We should teach our students to observe silence and practice meditation for their physical and spiritual growth. We are too much outward-bound. All of us watch and become the willing participants in the rat race. A saint like the master I had met looks like passé. My internal and external peace have both been shattered beyond repair. How right the master was in his thought and practice!

In 1983 when I was traveling in the Himalayas with some friends, we stopped at one of the temples on the river Ganges. My host asked me if I was interested in going inside the temple. I asked, "What's so special about this temple?" He said, "Oh, nothing special except that a great saint from your state was cremated near this temple."

When he told me his name, I immediately started climbing the steps of the temple. That was my master's final resting place when he left his mortal body. He had come all the way to the gorgeous and holy Himalayas to bid final farewell to the world.

I went inside his shrine. There was a big framed picture of him. When I looked at his picture, all the memories rushed back to me. He touched millions of lives. He showed the world how to lead a clean and productive life. His life was a message to all of his followers. I stood in silence for some time in front of his picture. Before I left, I put some fresh flowers under his picture. My host asked me surprisingly, "Mr. Tambe, did you know him?"

"Yes, he was the master I should have followed then. What a mistake! What a mistake!" I murmured to myself.

How I miss him now! I realize the importance of a great teacher. One great teacher is worth thousands of books and millions of dollars. How lucky I was to have an opportunity to sit down at his feet and listen to his words of wisdom! He showed me the noble path, but I didn't have the courage to follow him. Robert Frost wrote in his famous lines, "I shall be telling this with a sigh / Somewhere ages and ages hence/ Two roads diverge in a wood and / I took the one less traveled by, / And that has made all the difference". I didn't have the guts to take a different road, pay the price, and make the difference in my life. Now I realize that it is not always one's conscience but stark selfishness that makes cowards of us all.

A Unique American

ᐤ

Sometimes you read a novel and get the impression that the hero is simply fictitious. You could never find such a character in real life. But truth is at times shocking and you might be proven wrong. It happened to me when I finished reading Somerset Maugham's *The Razor's Edge.* I loved Maugham as writer because of his vivid characters and his international experience reflected in all his works. *The Razor's Edge* was my favorite because the story has an Indian spiritual background and should be very appealing to materially oriented Americans. (For that matter, Indians are no less materialistic!)

I read *The Razor's Edge* in my college days in India, and I never forgot Larry, the hero of his novel. Like most Americans, he is deeply soaked in materialism. His rich female friends are trying to hook him and tie his knot as soon as possible. But Larry is disgusted with their attitude toward their close friends who reflect the style of the rich and the powerful. They are simply cold and self-engrossed. He is frustrated in love. He is restless inside. There are more questions than answers in his life. During that time, he comes in contact with a person who suggests that he go to India to get answers to the questions that bother him. He departs to India in search of inner peace. He visits many places and meets saints and fakes there. Finally, he meets a man and finds the inner peace he was seeking. He comes back to the United States but is a changed man who understands his rich relatives and poor female friends. He has no attachment to material things, and he is totally in charge of his life. He is not interested marrying the rich girl to whom he was engaged. On the contrary, he feels sorry for her. No one understands him. He has more understanding and compassion for the people around him. But to his friends and relatives, he is an odd man out!

This is the summary of Maugham's *The Razor's Edge* as I recall it now. When I read the novel during my college days, I didn't believe a word of it, although I had enjoyed reading his works. I thought there is no Larry in real life. It was all Maugham's imagination.

In this case, the reality was more powerful and attractive than the fictional character. I never dreamed that I would ever meet such an unusual American in my life. In 1971, I read an article on Richard Alpert, who taught at Harvard and during the 1960s. He was expelled from Harvard because it was found that he had experimented with psychedelic drugs such as LSD, which were illegal. Because he was experimenting with deadly drugs to get a kick and reach the unknown, his friend suggested that he go to India and find a guru (a mentor) to get answers to his questions. He went to India and after a long haul in the Himalayas, he met an old man sitting on the heap of dust. He was basking in the tender rays of the sun smoking his *Hukka* (a water tobacco pipe). He looked at Richard and asked, "Young man, are you through with your LSD experiments?"

Richard was shocked. How did this old man know that he had experimented with drugs at Harvard when he was sitting at the foot of the Himalayas? It was beyond his comprehension. He said to himself, "This is the man I was looking for all my life. I am glad I found him after a long search. I have got to know his secrets. He alone can answer my questions that have been haunting me for years."

He went to him and politely asked him how in the world he knew who he was and what he had done in America to find inner peace.

"There are many things a person can know by sitting at one place. He does not have to go to America to find out what's going on there. I can read your mind like a book by sitting here. It's like watching TV at home."

To cut a long story short, Richard became his follower and learned many things about this man called Neem Karoli Baba ("Maharaj-ji") and his teaching about life and God. He came back to Boston to meet his family. He life had changed 180 degrees. He was at peace with himself (like Larry in *The Razor's Edge*).

Richard came from a very rich family. His father wanted him to make lots of money in business and settle down with a nice rich girl. Richard was not at all interested in money and family life. He was interested in human beings, and he was determined to serve them for the rest of his life. That was going to be his mission. No wonder his parents were terribly disappointed at his decision. (They must have cursed India in the hearts.) Richard changed his name from Richard Alpert to Baba Ram Dass, which means the servant of god, the Hindu god, Ram. He bought an old Volkswagen and traveled all over America in his simple Indian dress, giving lectures on the heritage of India and exhorting young people to get involved in the service of humankind. He started the Hanuman Foundation to help the poor and the powerless in this country.

I met Baba Ram Dass at Chapel Hill in the 1970s when he came to talk to students at the University of North Carolina. I had read his books *Be Here Now* and *Grist for the Mill*. The hall was full. There were a handful of people from India. Apart from reading his books, most of the Indians had not even heard his name. I was profoundly impressed by his simplicity, his dedication to the cause, and his deep knowledge of Indian mythology. When he talked, the audience was spellbound. In the post–Vietnam War era, he appealed to the young people more. They had not yet been exposed to the gospel of profit preached and practiced by Ronald Reagan. Not the outside material world but the inside spiritual world still held sway over the minds of the young. They were struggling hard to find answers (like Richard did in his early days) to questions that unsettled their minds.

After the speech, I went on the dais to introduce myself and talk to him briefly. When he learned that I was from India and had also taught in the Peace Corps, he advised me, "Mr. Tambe, India is a great country in the spiritual and philosophical sense. She needs you more now. Go back and serve your own people." I didn't want to discuss my personal problems with him and tell him why I was living in America. I bowed down in an Indian style and left.

For many years I have been reading articles on Baba Ram Dass and his constructive work at his resort in New Mexico. I was deeply saddened to read that in 1997, he had a stroke and is now confined to wheelchair in California. The doctors thought he was going to die soon. But he has survived all odds and is totally in charge of his mental faculties. At the age of seventy, he is still teaching and touching many lives.

My fascination for Baba Ram Dass has not receded. In fact over the years, it has grown. He is not a religious but a spiritual leader who has encouraged people to reexamine their lives and values and dedicate themselves to the service of mankind. I have come to love and respect him more, especially now when so many religious leaders in India and America have been surrounded by sex and money scandals. Through his example he has shown how a public leader should behave and lead the people to win their trust. No wonder he is an unusual American!

"I found wisdom in silence," says Baba Ram Dass.

THE LAST TEMPTATION

As much as the Western mind is impressed by the painting *The Last Supper,* so is my Eastern mind with the painting *The Temptation,* based on the final break of Lord Buddha with his family before he embarked on his journey for the search for truth.

In *The Temptation,* the painter has very skillfully brought out the emotional status and the wavering mind of Buddha when he looks at his wife and son sleeping quietly in bed in the royal palace. He has made up his mind to renounce this world, and he is more determined than ever to find answer to the nature of the ultimate reality. But at the last moment, he is tempted to give a final kiss to his only son. He takes steps toward the boy but stops short. He thinks if he kisses his son he might wake up his wife and his plan to leave the family will wither away. He controls himself and avoids the great temptation of kissing his son for the last time.

I am sure a storm must have raged in Buddha's mind at that moment. He must have been terribly torn inside between the spiritual world and the material world. What factors and considerations did he have to encounter before he embarked on his final journey? Only he knows about the pains in his agonizing decision. We can only guess. (Does any one know what thoughts crossed Christ's mind when he was being crucified?) It would be a fascinating study to find out the mental struggle such great minds go through when they undertake such a tortuous journey.

Buddha was born a prince. At the time of his birth, after studying his horoscope, a court astrologer had predicted that he would either be one of the greatest kings in India or one of the greatest saviors of mankind on earth. Because his father did not cherish the idea of his son renouncing the world and becoming a saint, he decided to take every precaution to keep all misery and sadness out of the boy's sight.

Despite his best efforts, he didn't succeed. One day while taking a stroll with a servant, Buddha saw an old lady outside the palace carrying on her head a stack of wood. She was bent like a bow when she carried the wood. Her face was wrinkled, She was using a cane. There were wrinkles on her hands and feet, too. "What has happened to this lady and why?" Buddha asked his servant. He was told that when people get old, they become weak in body and mind. Their bodies are pestered with wrinkles.

Ten minutes later Buddha saw a man being carried over the shoulders of four men, fully wrapped and tied to bamboo and accompanied by a large crowd. Some of them were weeping loudly and chanting the name of god, some throwing flowers over the body of the dead man.

Buddha didn't understand what was going on. He queried his servant again and asked for an explanation. "Sire, this is the end of life. All of us have to depart from this world one day. Some leave early and some late. But death comes to all of us, irrespective of class, creed, or our social positions. Those who are born must die. That's the law of nature, and nobody can defy it."

Buddha was terribly upset over the condition of the old lady and the death of the man. He asked himself how it could be avoided. He said to himself, "There must be a solution to it." He wanted to make the difference not only in his life but also in the lives of others by finding a solution to the eternal problem troubling humanity. His mind was made up. He was going to leave behind his family and his kingdom and cut off all ties that bound him to this mundane world. He was going to lose a lot to gain something more precious in the lives of human beings.

He was standing on the threshold—the dividing line between this world and the spiritual world. He was attracted to his wife, his only son, and the kingdom he was going to inherit after his father's death. But Buddha set aside all the temptations that had chained him to this world. His mind was made up. He was going to renounce the world and undertake his journey to find the nature of reality. He had to overcome all obstacles. To do so, he had to pass his first test: leaving his close family for ever!

Buddha left his family, became enlightened, and founded a new religion. He came out with a Code of Conduct (the Golden Rules) to follow to lead a good life on this earth and for the realization of Nirvana (the state of absolute blessedness)!

What can we learn from the temptation of Buddha and his search for truth?

First, like Buddha, all of us are always tempted one time or another in our lives. Do we have the resolution of Buddha to conquer it so that we can realize our ultimate aim in life? We see old people every day and witness dead people from time to time. We see and then forget. We don't examine our own lives in the light of the observed events in life. It's a hard task, and one in a million passes the test as Buddha did. That's what makes the difference in our lives and sometimes in the lives of others. The painting of a temptation is a constant reminder to all of us what we ought to do when faced with temptations in life.

TWO FACES: MAHATMA AND HIS MURDERER

I do not remember the exact year when Mahatma Gandhi passed through my city of Baroda, India.* I was a teenager in a high school at the time. There was a lot of excitement in our city because the people were very anxious to have a look at this great leader. This was going to be once-in-a-lifetime opportunity. They wouldn't want to miss seeing the man who had changed the face of India and had shaken the very roots of the mighty British empire with his unique method of nonviolence.

It was a very cold December morning. People from the neighboring villages and towns had assembled near the railway station. Some had climbed on trees and tall buildings to have a good look at the leader who had struck chord in their hearts. We had learned that Gandhi was on his way to Bombay to attend the meeting of the National Congress Party.

When the train arrived in the station at two in the morning, people started shouting slogans—"Long live Mahatma Gandhi! We want to see Mahatmaji." I was far away from the crowd and the railway station, standing in a corner under the tree. There was no chance for me to look at this great man. People were getting restless because there was no sign of him coming out to greet the surrounding crowd. He was fast asleep in his berth!

Gandhi was a very disciplined person. He went to bed exactly at ten at night and, irrespective of season, got up at four in the morning. He observed fasting and silence on every Monday. Gandhi was informed by his secretary that the train would not leave the station because some people were lying on the railway tracks to stop the train so they can have a look at him! People had given the leader the taste of his nonviolent medicine! Reluctantly, he came out at the railway compartment door with folded hands. Obviously, he had not appreciated the people's gesture that upset his routine schedule. People shouted the slogan "Long live Gandhiji!" He made no speech but quietly went back to bed.

Why did people behave the way they did? They really loved and respected him. Indians had never seen such a leader who had so identified himself with the toiling masses. He lived like them and dressed like them. Not only that, he went a step forward. He did what no other Indian leader had done before. He started *living* among the untouchables in the capital of India, New Delhi! No wonder the late prime minister of Great Britain Winston Churchill described him as "a naked fakir!"

I didn't get the chance to see him, and I was terribly disappointed. But to be present there was itself an unforgettable experience for me. To me, Gandhi was the most powerful leader who held no political power or position. His real power came from the grass roots, the masses of India.

My second memory of Mahatma Gandhi is very tragic and painful. I will never forget it as long as I live. It was January 30, 1948. I had come home from school and was relaxing with a cup of hot tea when my neighbor came on bicycle and shouted to his brother from the street, "Good news, brother. Gandhi shot dead in New Delhi!" I couldn't believe my ears. I knew it was false. The neighbor who broke the news never liked Gandhi or his politics. In fact, they had hated him all their lives, and their like-minded fellows had tried to kill him many times.

I ran to the streets and found that the shocking news was indeed true. People started closing their shops to show respect to the departed leader. I saw a few old people and women crying and sobbing in streets.

Later, I recalled that the man who had assassinated Gandhi had visited my neighbor three or four weeks before. I thought I had seen this murderer when he went to bathroom downstairs. The tragedy of my life was that, despite my best efforts, I could not see the face of the Mahatma, but accidentally I did see the face of an assassin who ended the life of a simple man who harmed nobody in the world! How do you explain this tragic situation to anyone?

Notes

* On Mahatma Gandhi

1. Gandhi, M. K., *An Autobiography: The Story of My Experiments With Truth*. Boston: Beacon Press, 1957.

2. Gandhi, M. K., *Collected Works of Mahatma Gandhi*. Vols 1–90. Ahmedabad: Navajivan Trust, 1967–1984.

3. Jack, Homer A., "M. K. Gandhi and Martin Luther King, Jr." *Mahatma Gandhi: 100 Years*. S. Radhakrishnan (ed.). New Delhi: Gandhi Peace Foundation, 1968.

4. Pyarelal, *Mahatma Gandhi: The Last Phase*. Vols 1 & 2. Ahmedabad: Navajivan Publishing House, 1956.

5. Cousins, Norman (ed.), *Profiles of Gandhi*. Delhi: Indian Book Company, 1969.

PURITY AND DIVINITY

These days it has become a fashion among religious preachers to delude people into thinking that anyone can realize god if they follow their advice. And who are these people? They are gurus like the late Rajneesh from India and a doctor with Indian origin, Deepak Chopra, who is providing tips through books and lectures on the methods of God realization. Our Christian crusaders, like Jimmy Swaggart, Jim Bakker, Oral Roberts, and others are not far behind. In the name of God, they are misleading the people. To amass wealth in the name of religion (a better word is *prostituting*) is the name of the their game. Both these Eastern and Western preachers are tarred with the same brush except that religious leaders like Rajneesh and Chopra are deeply knowledgeable about their religious craft and Eastern philosophy. Both are great communicators. I have no quarrel with their knowledge or their communication skills.

My problem is with their lifestyle and their premise that God and money can coexist. Rajneesh lived a luxurious life with more than ninety Rolls Royces at his command and a huge ranch in Oregon for his followers. Deepak Chopra lives in a $ 2 million home in Malibu, charging large fees for his lectures, selling his books and cassettes, and preaching how God can be seen on this earth. Both are super salesmen.

I do not know any saint, living or dead, in India or here who realized God by minting money. Those who have truly realized God in the East and the West have always stayed away from money. They know that money and material wealth keeps people away from God. They are the biggest obstacles in the path of God-realization. So they have literally followed the Bible dictum, "Thou shall not worship God and mammon." Christ put it beautifully when he warned the money-lenders that it is easier for a camel to enter the eye of a needle than a rich man to enter heaven. How true!

I have written about my master in India who never touched money all his life. The same was the case with another India's famous saint, Ramakrishna. He never cared for or touched money in his entire life. They knew very well that money is one of the greatest barriers in the path of God-realization. Purity in life enjoins the need from staying away from wealth. Lord Buddha left behind his kingdom to realize the kingdom of heaven within.

Among the Ten Commandments in the Bible, my favorite is, "Blessed are those who are pure at heart, for they shall see God." The emphasis is on purity. There cannot be any clearer message than this. Still, religious leaders try to combine God and gold and exploit religion for their own material benefits. Pat Robertson, the famous TV evangelist, has built an evangelical empire not only in America but also in Liberia, Africa. Instead of helping the poor who have very little education and a staggering 85 percent unemployment, there he is exploring for oil to make money! Such self-styled servants of God give religion and God a bad name. There is no way they can ever see God. Not in this life and with this kind of their lifestyle, nor in the afterlife. These religious leaders underestimate the divine intelligence of God Almighty. It is easier to fool the simple folks on earth than to do so to the Heavenly Father.

There is another dimension about purity that is often missed by the general public but deliberately neglected by the practitioners of religion. It is that God and sex also cannot coexist. It's like mixing oil and water. Let us go back to India's famous preacher, -Rajneesh. During the 1960s and the early part of 1970s, his message of "self-realization through sex" was an appealing message to the so-called flower children. He was terribly wrong on this thesis. I know that there is a religious sect in India that believes and practices it. But they are not in the mainstream of Indian philosophy or religion. I have read books by Rajneesh and benefited from them. He was a great scholar and a wonderful communicator. His command over the language and depth of scholarship were very impressive. But his lifestyle in America and his distortion of the India philosophy turned me off.

Saints in India have come down hard on money and sex, affirming that both are stumbling blocks in the path of God-realization. Ramakrishna once remarked to his students that a religious man should always be checked during the day and the night as well! How true! Our preachers have slept with prostitutes and have openly indulged in homosexual behavior with teenagers in their churches. These so-called men of God have betrayed people's trust in them and the trust of the church. One does not get nearer to God by donning a monk's robe or using the pulpit to make speeches every Sunday. One's transparent behavior, demonstrated compassion, and selfless service to the poor puts one in proximity to God. Nothing else counts.

The question then is why do people give money and follow those religious crooks? It's an age-old riddle. It seems that people have been fooled in all ages, and religious leaders will continue to do so unless their followers expose them in public and teach them a good lesson.

GANDHI FOR OUR TIMES

It happened in 1922. Gandhi was being tried in the British court in India for his defiance of the British law. When the judge pronounced the sentence, he observed, "Mr. Gandhi, you are a great man. You are ethical and very honest in public life. But as a judge I am not concerned with the ethical side of the law. I am bound by laws made by the government. I have to interpret the laws and apply them in your case. It's my duty." He sentenced Gandhi to rigorous imprisonment.

Here is the tragedy of our government and the people that support it. Neither the judge nor the government that appointed him was concerned with the ethics of the law. The question of justice rarely crosses the minds of our rulers when they are in power.

This is the story of not only of the British who ruled India then but also the unfortunate story of all governments who, in the name of the law, indulge in injustice and cause harm to millions of individuals. It is not only the government but also individuals like you and me who throw ethics to winds to serve our day-to-day purposes. Politicians do it, and business-people are unbeatable in this art of bending ethics to make a fast buck.

What is going to happen to society if we keep indulging in unethical behavior to realize our material goals? I am sure we can prosper materially and start rotting spiritually. Do we really care for ethical values? Do we really want to nurture our souls? I think we know the answer to it. In the tug-of-war between God and money, we are already on the side of money. No wonder we are paying a heavy price for it. We have sowed the seeds of our social discontent and permanent decay.

Leaders like Gandhi show us the way to our social progress and inner happiness. But our selfishness makes us blind. We crush our conscience and take the wrong route. When will it end? If we take this road, how will it impact the next generation? If we care for the future of our children, we have to consider the ethical side of life and set an ideal example. Then and only then can we say we are good role models for them. Children are smart and can easily see through our games. Once their trust in us is shattered, there is no way to get back.

KNOWING AND DOING IT

❧

There is a beautiful story in the Indian epic *The Mahabharat*. It is a story about a great battle fought between two families over a kingdom. All compromises to avoid the battle and the bloodshed were explored. One final attempt was made by Drupad, and elderly relative of Duryodhana, who was a powerful but cruel ruler of the Pandawa family. Drupad goes to Duryodhana and tries to convince him with reason that battle was no solution and if it occurred, both families would suffer tremendous losses. He appeals to his conscience but in vain.

Duryodhana listens to him attentively and finally admits to that he, too, would like to avoid the battle that would engulf all, but he is helpless. The reply of Duryodhana to Drupad is not only the tragedy of his life but also the tragedy of us all. Duryodhan is a great warrior and also a great scholar. He thanks his relative for his noble advice but politely tells him, "I know what religion is, but I cannot practice it. I know what evil is, but I cannot give it up."

All of us know in the hearts what is good and what is evil. We can easily distinguish between the two but—and that's a big *but*—like Duryodhana, we are unable to practice it!

When I was student reading the Greek philosophers like Socrates and Plato, they always emphasized the role of reason in one's life. The governing principle was that to do right, one must know first what right is. The only method to find this was reason. Is it true? I don't think so. We know very well, most of the time, what is good and bad for us. Then the sixty-four million dollar question is: why don't we all act on our understanding of the truth? There enters Duryodhana. We certainly know what is good for us, but we do not want to practice it for a simple reason: our self-interest.

When it comes to protecting self-interest, we say good-bye to principles, friends, and families. Self-interest takes priority over all. This is the tragedy with most of us. I know there may be a few great individuals who do not fit into this pattern, but they are exceptions to the rule. Such individuals stay away from power, money, and prestige and are not involved in any kind of critical decision-making process that affects millions of other individuals.

All of us care deeply for our families and their welfare. The real question is: to what extent do we go to protect the interests of our families? Do we go to the extent of killing them so that we can have everything? Or de we stick to the principle of "live and let live"? The choice is ours. It's up to us to curtail self-interest and keep it under tight control so that others may not be harmed. This is the principle of live and let live.

LEADERS AND FOLLOWERS

❧

Nietzsche, a German philosopher, remarked that "the last Christian died on the cross." What he meant was that Christ had no followers. Nietzsche was pointing out the tragedy of great leaders. Leaders are more discredited by their own followers than by their own enemies. The followers of the leaders often become the worst enemies of their masters. This is a painful conclusion of history.

This is especially true for religious leaders. All we have to do is look at the present political situation or go back to the dark ages in Western history to understand the meaning of Nietzsche's remark. History tells us that many wars have been fought and millions killed in the name of religion. When India was partitioned in 1947, more than half a million Hindus and Muslims were killed because they had different religions and they did not trust one another. They had lived together in harmony for centuries, but the partition of the country had fanned the flames of religion. The political leaders on both sides lost their balance and broader perspective on humankind.

We are often reminded that religion never exhorts its followers to kill others and destroy the holy places of other religions. But reality is very different. The fanatical Hindus in India destroyed a mosque in 1992 and the power-drunk religious leaders in Afghanistan demolished ancient statues of Buddha. The Christian missionaries who use economic power and force in developing countries to convert the poor fall under the same category. This is all undertaken in the name of religion!

When religious leaders call on their followers to kill their enemies and declare a holy war "Jihad" against other religions, it becomes a religious travesty. Those religious leaders who proclaim at the top of their voices to their followers to become martyrs in the holy war and go to heaven not only distort religion but also misinterpret it. When religious leaders and their followers destroy temples, mosques, synagogues, churches, other places of worship, and statues of great religious leaders, they need to be condemned in the strongest sense of the word and some action (such as sanction) should be imposed on the country that shelters them. It is the job of the United Nations to take the initiative in this matter and put sense into the heads of religious nuts. Only a world community that believes in secular principles and respects all religions can do it.

Neither any religion nor its adherents can claim any sanctuary when they issue notices or Fatwas to kill any human being because he or she has criticized their religion. The heart of any religion is tolerance, and its soul is human sanctity. Religious leaders tell us that religion never teaches anyone to kill or harm others. But the followers of all religions indulge in violence and destroy sacred places of other religions and convert others.

Religion must be judged not on the basis of what is written in holy books but by what is being practiced by its followers. That should be its only measuring stick. The pious platitudes of their leaders and the generous interpretations of their holy books should not be accepted as an excuse for killing others and destroying holy places. Neither should the unpardonable religious acts of their followers be tolerated as acts of misadventure. Their religion must tell them to pause and ponder over their hideous and irreligious acts.

It's high time to warn religious fanatics and zealots that their behavior is disgusting and will not be tolerated by all freedom-loving people all over the world. We have put up with irreligious behavior for a long time. It's time and to act and tear off their masks in public.

THERE IS ALWAYS A SECOND CHANCE IN LIFE

Indian history is fascinating. Like most history books in the world, the history of India I had to study was distorted and one-sided. There was great emphasis on kings and queens, battles and bloodshed, treaties and treasons. Very little was written about the plight of the common people or what went into the minds of great kings, queens, or warriors when they were confronted with death. I didn't like to memorize the names of kings and historical facts. I thought they were not worth remembering, except in a few cases, such as Ashoka, whose first battle was his last.* Our teachers emphasized only the names of places and kings, rather than their importance and contributions. These items were important to them from the examination point of view. Critical thinking about historical characters or questioning the decisions made by our leaders were not encouraged. Our teachers were ill equipped with historical facts and much less in interpreting their significance. They were not interested in history, much less in making one.

Later I read books on world history written by Gibson, H. G. Wells, Will Durant, and many Indian scholars. I soon realized that most of the Indian history books written by British scholars and Indians alike were hopelessly prejudiced and terribly biased. They saw history in black and white only. There was no color between. Of course, there were a few exceptions.

There were two kings in Indian history who have impressed me for different reasons. In character, religion, and values, both were poles apart. In fact, there was nothing common between them. Still, I thought, they had a lesson for all of us.

First let me introduce a Mogul emperor who ruled India from 1658 to 1707. His name was Aurangzeb. He ruled India with an iron hand and was a religious fanatic. He taxed the Hindu population, who were in majority. Although an extremely able administrator, Aurangzeb used his absolute power to kill his own brothers and his enemies. He trusted no one, not even his own shadow!

He expanded his kingdom, amassed vast wealth, and ruled India almost fifty years. Unlike his grandfather Akabar, Aurangzeb was one Mogul king who spent many years in India but never identified with the people. He was a ruthless outsider to his subjects. When he died, very few Hindus had reason to shed tears. Aurabgzeb's deathbed confession makes a very sad reading. He is reported to have uttered when he was dying, "I know not who I am, where I shall go, or what will happen to this sinner full of sins—My years have gone by profitless. God has been in my heart, yet my darkened eyes have not recognized his light—There is no hope for me in the future. The fever is gone but only the skin is left—I have greatly sinned and know not what torments await me—May the peace of God be upon me."

Here is the tragedy of an able but a merciless king. He had everything in life except a sense of direction. His life was empty and meaningless. I thought Aurangzeb is the best example of what the Bible has so beautifully put, "What good is it to win the whole world and lose your own soul?" This king bartered away his own soul for thirty pieces of gold!

There is no question in mind that we are all sinners, some bigger than others. The difference is of degree only. But we always have an opportunity to turn our lives around and make it better. We *always* have a second chance in life.

Here is a shining example of a great, ancient king of India who completely changed his life. His name was Ashoka. He came to power in 273 B.C. in India. Will Durant describes Ashoka as a philosopher king. He was neither a philosopher nor a kind man in the beginning of his career as a ruler. In fact, this great king, who was to go down in history as one of the greatest kings of all time, acted more like a butcher when he came to the throne. Thousands of animals were slaughtered in his kingdom for food. Many of his prisoners who were condemned to suffer and die in his prison, which was described as "Ashoka's hell." He used all sorts of dreadful methods to torture his prisoners. The king had ordered the prison guards that no one who entered his prison must come out alive, and this applied to his prison guards, too!

But when Ashoka saw a Buddhist monk who was ordered to be burned alive and by some miracle would not burn, he had another look at his appalling life. At the same time, he also learned that his troops had won a great victory by conquering the neighboring state of Kalinga. He was informed by his commander-in-chief that they had to slaughter thousands of soldiers and innocent men and women there to ensure victory. After hearing of the bloody accounts from his soldiers, he visited the battlefield. The dead bodies and mangled parts made him cry and reexamine his life.

Ashoka started searching his own soul and asked himself, "What am I doing? And for what?" He immediately ordered his prisoners released and gave back the conquered territory of Kalinga with apology to the people. He shocked his own military officers. But his mind was made up. He was going to change his life for the better. He halted the killing of all animals in his state. He joined the Buddhist order and adopted the Buddhist religion, becoming a devout follower of the principles of nonviolence and peace. His kingdom became a sanctuary for birds and animals. He created a ministry to look after the welfare of aborigines and backward tribes. He even appointed a special officer to promote the education of women in his kingdom. Ashoka became an harbinger of peace and love. He practiced what Buddha calls the right conduct. Through his example, he showed how we can all change and turn around our lives.

No wonder the great British historian H. G. Wells describes Ashoka, "For eight and twenty years Ashoka worked sanely for the real needs of men. Amidst the tens of thousands of names of monarchs that crowd the columns of history, their majesties and graciousness and serenities and royal highnesses and the like, the name of Ashoka shines, and shines almost alone, a star. From Volga to Japan his name is still honored."

Ashoka changed his own life; Aurangzeb had a second chance but stuck to his old, cruel way of life as a king. On his deathbed, he realized that he was a great sinner. It was too late. Aurangzeb and Ashoka had different religious background as rulers. Both had the free will to change their lives. One did and the other was nearly unrepentant. Why? What strong factors motivate human beings to take such drastic action and stick to it?

I do know have answers to these questions. One thing is clear. We *can* change our lives if we want to. It is up to us to wreck our life like Aurangzeb or build our life for better like Ashoka. The choice is ours. We alone can make the difference in our lives.

Notes

* On Ashok

1. Ahir, D.C., *Ashok the Great.* Delhi: B.R. Publishing Co., 1995.
2. Kautily, Rangarajan L. N. (ed.), *The Arthashastra,* Delhi: Penguin India, 1992.
3. Thaper, R., *Ashok and the Decline of the Mauryas.* Oxford Press, 1961.
4. Mukerji, R.K., *Ashok.* Madras: Oxford Press, 1928.

NO ROSA, NO KING

After reading the life story of John Adams and his active wife, Abigail, I am firmly convinced that behind the success and glory of every man or a leader there is a woman who stands behind him through thick and thin and inspires him to greater heights.

This was true in the case of Dr. Martin Luther King Jr., who became famous all over the world as a great civil rights leader who carried on the struggle for economic freedom and constitutional rights of blacks. But it was Rosa Parks who dragged him out of the church pulpit in Montgomery, Alabama, to the main street where the poor blacks were fighting for human dignity.

Just think! If Rosa Parks had not refused to give up her front seat on the bus in Montgomery and like thousands of others had quietly gone to take her seat in the back of the bus on April 4, 1965, what would have happened? Dr. King would have continued to preach as a young pastor at the Montgomery Baptist church and probably would have made many fiery speeches to stir the souls of folks in his churches. His congregation would have applauded him and rewarded him with better salary and a house. But he would never have known to the world as a great human being and the one who trumpeted the grievances of the poor in America.

It was Rosa who inspired him to do God's work and get involved into the streets of downtown Montgomery, where the poor struggled hard to make their daily living. From all accounts, it seems that King had neither a desire to get involved in fighting for the rights of the poor blacks nor did he want to leave his pulpit preaching for the street struggle. Rosa made him search his soul and showed the real place of worship.

Rosa was firm and determined. She had a powerful message for the world. All she was looking for was an effective messenger who could articulate her message and play all across America. In King, she not only found a mighty messenger but also a communicator who sent her message to the whole world and made *Rosa* a household word.

All of us have personal experiences, good or bad, like Rosa. All of us get tired of sitting in the back seat. Most of us keep quiet or complain and once in a while raise our voice in protest. Seldom do we think to go beyond words or take up a fight for the rest of the suffering humanity. We have been conditioned into acting like Uncle Tom. We accept things as they are and leave it God Almighty to change it.

I do not know whether Rosa was inspired by Gandhi, who had similar experience in South Africa. Gandhi had a first-class railway ticket but was kicked out of the railway compartment when he protested and refused to leave his seat. Why? Because he was a colored man!

I am glad that there are some Gandhis and Rosas left in this world to show us the way human beings should act in this unjust world. They echo the message that injustice done somewhere is justice threatened everywhere. We have to unite and stand up to fight for our rights and the rights of others.

OUR JUDGMENT ROD

Many years back, when I taught Peace Corps members who were India-bound, we emphasized the cultural differences between India and America and the need for cultural under-standing and appreciation of other cultures. To our great sur-prise, we found that the trained Corps members forgot the les-son and expressed shock and started criticizing the Indians about their social mores and unhealthy living habits when they arrived. During this time, a Peace Corps member working in an African country criticized the open bath system and con-veyed his views to his friend on a postcard. Unfortunately the postcard fell into the hands of an American reporter, and it was published in a newspaper. It created an international stir and the Peace Corps volunteer had to be recalled immediately.

This is a classic example how we do injustice to the peo-ples of other countries by judging them by our own cultural rod. Americans think we are superior to others because we have money to burn and we are the most powerful country in the world. This is why other countries call us "ugly Americans." The late Senator William Fulbright (Arkansas) in his Senate floor speech remarked that Americans suffer from the disease called American arrogance.

All cultures have good and bad things in them. Why can't we appreciate the bright side of any culture and take it as it is?

We talk about the rainbow culture of humankind, but in reality we pass judgment on other people and their different ways of life. I remember vividly an incident that happened at my home in America. One day when I was eating on my dining table with my hands (most Indians eat that way), my American friend walked in. He was shocked to see me eating with my hands. He asked me why I was eating with my hands instead of spoons and forks. I told him that's the way I had been eating since my boyhood days. He had a hard time believing it. Luckily, he did not pass a judgment on me.

There is a cultural gap among nations, and it needs to be filled with cultural understanding and communication. All cultures have bright and dark sides. The cultural differences should be understood and appreciated by the people concerned. There is no such things as superior or inferior culture. It's only *different*. Our attitude toward other cultures plays a vital role in cultivating or destroying relations with other cultures. If we fail to understand the culture of the host country, we may lose their business or cost us lives and a lot of money. One American diplomat remarked on the Viet Nam War that America lost because of its failure to understand the culture of Viet Nam. We failed to understand them, and we judged them the wrong way. That war cost $30 billion and 58,000 lives, one of the costliest mistakes our politicians ever made. We need to build cultural bridges among nations and stop passing judgments on them because they are different in color, language, and natural resources.

CLASS AND VALUES

Many of us have a skewed notion that lower-class people have lower values and their values, compared with upper-class values, are very different. What is implied here is that lower-class people are dishonest and will always cheat to serve their purpose.

I am not a sociologist to make a value judgment on this. But as a member of the middle class, I believe that we are wrong in assuming that the values of the upper or the middle class are superior to those of the lower classes. I do not believe for a moment that superior values are a monopoly of the upper/middle class. Values are not necessarily correlated to any class. They are individual-oriented. I found this out during a recent visit to India.

I attended a wedding ceremony of one of my relatives in my city. To remain in touch with my friends and family members, I had carried a cell phone I had recently purchased there. According to Indian standards, it was a luxury and naturally cost me a good bit. After three hours, when I returned home by auto-rickshaw (a popular Indian vehicle that runs on gas-oil combination) I suddenly realized that I had lost my cell phone. I immediately dashed back and checked with my relatives, but to no avail. I couldn't find the phone. I was mad at myself because of my poor memory. I had replaced the battery the day before and renewed my contract with the company for the next two years to save money. Now this was all down the drain. I had lost not only the cell phone but looked bad in the eyes of my relatives. Everybody asked the same stupid question, "How could he do it?" They knew that I was used to a cell phone in America. One sarcastically remarked, "It's hard to believe that a man with Ph.D. has such a bad memory!"

I couldn't sleep well that night. I had made an expensive mistake, and I cursed myself many times.

The next day when I was having my breakfast, somebody knocked at the front door. When I opened it, I saw two young men in workers' clothes. They spoke in Hindi, which I understood well. I didn't know the purpose of their visit. Meanwhile, my son had joined us. He immediately recognized those two people. They were the rickshaw drivers who had driven us to the wedding location the previous night. My son asked them the purpose of their visit. They brought out the cell phone from a pocket and asked me if it belonged to me. They had found it in their rickshaw when they left us last night.

I could not believe my eyes that those illiterate but honest people had come to return my phone. I later learned that they had taken a lot of trouble to locate our house. I was touched and impressed by their transparent honesty. I offered them tea and asked my son to reward them with some cash. I really wanted to find out about their background that motivated them to make such a noble gesture. They could have sold my phone and made good money. They told me they didn't know how to use it and get in touch with me. Finally, they relied on their memory to visit they way they had come the previous night.

While they were having tea with us, I learned that they came from North India (I lived on the west coast) from the holy city of Benaras. They looked on the River Ganges as their mother. While they were in Benaras, they bathed in it daily. Their parents taught them to be good human beings and lead a clean life, keeping mother Ganges in mind all the time. I have some educated friends who have lived in Benaras for years but are not half as honest as these two people. They came from the lower class. They had taken a loan from the local bank to buy the rickshaw to make an honest living. Poor, but incorruptible! How come?

Before they left, I told both of them that if they needed any letter of recommendations for a bank or any employment services in future, I would be glad to provide it.

Where do people get such honesty in their lives? Is it trust in God that makes them honest? They certainly practiced what they had learned from religion and they did listen to their mother, the Ganges! I firmly believe that the individual, not the class, that makes the difference! This incident renewed my faith in humanity. I was glad to find that there are still some honest people left in a world rocked by corruption.

HOLIER THAN THOU

When I was in India, I had a classmate whose father was a jail warden. As part of his job, this man had to witness executions of condemned men in a state prison. Generally the day after it happened, my friend would tell us the horrible story with a graphic description what happened to the man when he was hanged. His tongue came out a foot long and his eyes were socked out. Before the execution, he asked for forgiveness, et cetera. My friend would narrate the whole incident as if he, not his father, was an eye-witness. After hearing such a horrible story, I would not feel like eating lunch in the afternoon.

Death by hanging! How does a condemned man feel when he is about to be hanged? Does he really repent for his sins? Is death the only way to punish human beings? Could we not keep them in a jail for the rest of their lives, if needed, and give them a second chance for rehabilitation? Do we have a moral right to take some one's life because he had committed a heinous crime? How different are we when we execute a person in the name of law and order? Two different criteria for two different people? Don't people change after years, as historians and psychologists tell us? Finally, should people who live in glass houses throw stones at the prison cell of a condemned man? How righteous are we? It seems that our politicians who believe in the death penalty are governed more by the biblical saying of "an eye for an eye" principle rather than the "thou shall not kill" commandment. And these are all honorable men!

I am proud of our beautiful state of North Carolina. But we are fast becoming the number one state in executing people. Right now (in 2003) the state of Texas is number one in executing the highest number of prisoners. It's the home state of our president, George W. Bush.

No person or government has a moral right to take anyone's life, even though it be legally sanctioned. I agree there may be some exceptions to killing somebody during a war or in self-defense. I am not 100 percent a Quaker or a Gandhian to adhere to the principle of nonviolence without an exception.

As a teacher who has taught for many years, I firmly believe that it is better to open a school and close a prison. What is shocking is the fact that in the United States, the government is spending three times more money on a prisoner behind bars than on a student in the classroom! What we are doing in the name of law is unpardonable. When conservative presidents like Ronald Reagan and George Bush Sr. came to power, to placate the extremist elements in their party, they whole-heartedly supported the death penalty. They were brainwashed with the idea that executing a man or a woman is the easiest way to solve the crime problem. Reagan acted in too many western movies and perhaps believed in the solution of hanging. Richard Nixon was first elected on law and order issue. And he was the one who broke the law and encouraged his Cabinet members to break it. He was the only president who had to resign in office to avoid impeachment. We have one set of rules for our rulers and another for our convicts. Obviously, they are not equal in the eyes of the law.

Research does not support the death penalty as a workable solution for crime. The death penalty does not even deter crime. It's cruel and useless. We have to look to other humane forms of punishment. I do not defend the killers at all. But I cannot justify the legal killing of convicted felons by any state or a country. When we kill anybody, we degrade humanity. What happened to our Christian values of love and forgiveness? God gives life, and only He alone has a right to take it away. Only He has the divine intelligence to understand all and see clearly through the motives of all human beings. It is His right, not ours. The irony of it is that those who are for life and saving unborn babies are the first to demand death penalty for convicted criminals! Think!

WRONG PLACE, WRONG ADVICE

When my wife died, in India in 2000, a lot of our friends and relatives turned up at the condolence meeting to pay their respects to her. Needless to say, I was terribly shaken. I was hardly in a mood to talk to anybody, but I mustered enough courage to thank everybody for coming to express their sympathy.

Some of my elderly relatives really made me angry by trying to console me the wrong way. One came and hug me and remarked, "I know it's a terrible personal loss to you. But aren't you glad to know that, like many others, she didn't stay in bed for years and suffered but died suddenly with heart attack?" Whatever the age of the deceased person may be or the manner of the death, one's relatives want to be with the person for many more years. Death does not make any sense to them. I was wrapped up in sweet memories of my wife. I was not in a mood to listen to any unsolicited and unwanted advice from anyone who hardly came to see her when she was alive

Another close friend took my hand and whispered in my ear, "You know all of us have die one of these days. Why waste time on crying?" I was mad at him, too, but considering the solemn occasion, I controlled my anger and turned away.

Don't people realize that occasion like this demand seriousness? It is better at such times to keep quiet or hold a hand to share the sorrow of the bereaved person. But to offer advice like a philosopher (and they are not) serves no purpose. Instead of sharing sorrow, it only irritates the person whose wound is still fresh and has not yet started to heal. Time is the best healer.

I like the system of presenting flowers to express and share sorrow with the bereaved family. I think beautiful flowers speak louder than the actions and unwarranted presence of friends and relatives. A bouquet of flowers is worth tons of empty words. It lifts up the spirit of the person and nurtures the deep wound. I think it is also not a bad idea to present a book, like Marcus Aurelius's *Meditations;* his observations on life still make great sense. I would also consider giving a gift on such occasion a Hindu holy book, the *Bhagavad Gita,* which sheds ample light on life, death, and duty in life. The last thing a bereaved person needs on such occasions is the empty advice.

THE REAL CRIMINALS

When I was a student in India, my favorite teacher often used to quote, "Open a school and close a prison." There was a poem on *prison.* The poet had criticized the society for its attitude toward criminals and finally concluded that it is society through its legal system that creates hardened criminals and strengthens prison walls. My teacher liked the poem very much, and he would emphasize the point that all of us need to change our attitudes toward prisoners.

In my school days in India, the only time I had seen prisoners was when they would come in our city to sell vegetables with chains around their feet and hands. They wore saffron dress and were always accompanied by a warden, who collected money and supervised them with a gun.

In America, I visited many prisons, including a women's prison in Raleigh, North Carolina. I always compared them with the prisoners I had seen in India. But I never dreamed that I would have a face-to-face experience with a criminal.

Some years back, I needed a person to work in my garden to remove heavy stones and wood. I was looking for a worker who was strong, reliable, and not too expensive. Finally, I found Harry, a worker who was a heavy-built and tall and accustomed to hard work. He worked during the afternoon and ate lunch with my family. We liked his work and treated him like a member of our family. I use to pay him by the hour and paid him at the weekend.

Sometimes my friends would ask me to suggest a good and reliable and inexpensive worker to work in their garden or fix their leaking gutters or do some carpentry work. Harry would go to my friends' places and took care of their problems. They also seemed to be pleased with his mild manners and reasonable rates. Some called me to thank me for recommending such an excellent worker. I was also glad that I could be of some help to them.

One day I got a call from a friend, and he was terribly angry. It took me some time to understand his anger. He asked me if I had seen the local evening news. I had been too busy that evening to watch the news. He told me in angry tone that Harry had been arrested for raping a woman. And they blamed *me* for recommending a criminal to them.

It came as shock. How could that be? I immediately called the Harry's stepfather, who also had worked for me. He confirmed the news and told me he didn't want to talk about it. A week after the incident, I got a call from Harry's girlfriend requesting me to come to the court as a witness for Harry. I wanted to talk to Harry first. His girlfriend drove me to the prison where he was locked up. I learned that Harry had a criminal record that he had never revealed to me. When I met briefly in the lobby of the prison, his face was crestfallen. He looked ashamed for having hidden his dark past from me. I listened to his side of the story. I agreed to go to court as a witness on the condition that I would only talk about his work.

I can say from my experience that he was a hard and honest worker. He was always polite and courteous. But what disturbed me the most was the attitude of my close friends. The moment they knew that he was arrested for rape, they raised a ruckus against him and blamed me for recommending him to them. As if *I* had committed a great crime. The attitude of my friends changed suddenly after the revelation that he was a criminal. They made me sick. But as far as my experience with him was concerned, he was honest and trustworthy.

If we don't help to rehabilitate people like Harry, where else will they go? If they don't find honest work, will they not rob banks and indulge in burglary? Somebody has to give them a second chance for their rehabilitation. Think!

THE DIVINE RADAR

God doesn't discriminate. He believes in equal educational opportunities for all. He gives ample time to all of us to fit
into his spiritual image. Our Maker wants us to behave and
act in the right way so that our lives will be enriched individ-
ually and spiritually.

The question is often asked is: How do you know that
you are doing the "right" thing? The answer to that question
is very simple. God has put a divine radar in the heart of all
human beings. Every time we commit a sin or an immoral or
illegal act, our conscience or the divine radar instantly warns
us that it is wrong and we should not do it. For example,
when we try to cheat Uncle Sam on income taxes, perhaps
our conscience speaks up and tells us that what we are about
to do is wrong and should not do it. Even in small instances,
like making copies of your private documents on your office
machines or telling a lie to your boss on some occasions, your
conscience pinches you right away. The voice is raised in
protest. We are warned.

Have you not yourself experienced it sometimes? Of course
you have. This is the dividing line between a sinner and a saint.
The saints follow their divine radars to maintain purity in their
lives, but most of us follow the beaten path of sinning, which
enriches us in the material sense but impoverishes ours lives

spiritually. All of us have a choice. The devil never makes you do anything; we volunteer ourselves to do the devil's dirty work.

We *can* learn to heal our wounds before it's too late. We know too well what needs to be done. The inner conflict goes on in all human hearts and, unfortunately, most of the time the material side defeats the spiritual side. This happens every hour, every day. What can we do? How can we be on the right side of angels? The answer is very simple.

Follow your divine radar. Pray to God to give you spiritual strength to make the right decision. You will be surprised you will get help from Him. You will make the right decisions and come out a winner. How can we activate this divine radar? Simple: All of us can activate it through *purity*. The highest goal in life is that of purity of mind, purity of body, and purity in speech. The most difficult to practice is purity of mind. Unless your mind is totally in control, you cannot achieve it.

There are two dimensions of purity that most of us can practice if they are sincere. Purity is a spiritual process of cleansing ourselves of toxic elements that destroy our souls. We need to use a filter to purify ourselves. For example, we should stop telling lies that hurt others, stop interfering in somebody else's life for our own selfish ends, and stop denying others their basic rights as human beings. Life is not a soap opera show. When we violate nature's rules, it hurts us and others. All religions and saints have been telling us about it for centuries. For example, just read the Ten Commandments or Buddha's Golden Rules for clean living.

The positive side is much more important. Great leaders like Christ and Buddha, Socrates and Gandhi, have spelled it out in their own way. Christ calls it love; Buddha uses the term compassion. Gandhi calls it truth and nonviolence. Mother Teresa shows the way to serve human beings through service. Take your own pick and start purifying yourself now. Get rid of the toxic elements in your body and mind and develop the habit of leading a clean life. Do you want to do it or pigeon-hole your conscience? It's your choice. Remember: You alone can make that difference.

UNDERSTANDING VALUES

During the past thirty years there has been a lot of discussion on the understanding and applications of values in public life. This is especially true about education because American people and their leaders sincerely believe that everything starts from education. No wonder our late President Lyndon B. Johnson turn to education (he was himself a teacher) to fight the war on poverty.

We currently have a problem with our value system. Cheating in schools and colleges is on the rise. Cheating the government to avoid paying taxes has become a way of life. To top it all, politicians of both parties, instead of becoming role models, have frequently become the worst examples of demoralized behavior. Some of them are having affairs with members of their staffs, and some have sex in their offices! They go to churches and cheat the public. How can they talk about values? And who would listen to them?

When it comes to values, children in schools have become the greatest victims. They have become rudderless. They have no direction and are drifting aimlessly in the currents of materialism and selfishness. Some schools are now offering courses in values with the hope that it will improve the students' characters. But we have to understand the nature and working of values.

First, values are caught, not taught. My grandmother and my father never gave me a lecture on values, but they showed through their examples, how values should be practiced. My grandmother loved all human beings, birds, beasts, and plants. She worshiped them. I did not understand her behavior then. But as I look back, I fully understand her behavior and the hidden message behind it. She taught me to love living and inanimate objects. She could not read or write but taught me a valuable lesson in human relations.

My father, who was a schoolteacher, taught me to help all. He took care of the members of his family, including one of his brothers, who was blind. He gave shelter to a young widow who was not related to him. He was an obliging individual. I learned the lesson of helping others from him. Through his example he showed how it should be done. Helping others who were in distress was in his very soul.

These examples show that values are passed on, not taught. But the person who receives the values must be eager to know them and, more important, be committed to practice them. The giver and the receiver are both important elements in the value system.

Second, *values* is a relative term. What is valuable to you may be trash to someone else. Each person puts a premium on values. There is no point in passing judgment on the values of others because their values are different.

Whatever the values, material or spiritual, they are always dominated by self-interest. The ideology is no consideration of values when it comes to self-interest. Experiments in human behavior have confirmed this. Otherwise how can one explain the sad phenomenon of children killing their own schoolmates and forgetting the values they learned?

Finally, the best time and place of learning values is home. The best time to implant values among our kids is in early childhood. Still, it's no guarantee that it will work. Just do your duty and don't forget this; even the best parents have children who violate the values of the family, and others have children who cherish human values and pass on the heritage to their own children.

BEATING ABOUT THE BUSH

⌒

The worst part of American culture is its love affair with guns. I can understand that during the pioneering days, the frontiersmen lived by the gun and died by the gun at an early age. (The average life expectancy was only twenty-seven!). But why should we continue to live in violence in the new millennium? It's beyond the comprehension of my Eastern mind. To secure a right to protect themselves and kill others who trample on that right, Americans amended the constitution. The second amendment is the right to bear arms, which has delighted the members of the National Rifle Association.

Too often we watch on TV and read in the newspapers the schoolchildren are being killed by their schoolmates. Innocent by-standers become victims. Property worth millions is destroyed in the shooting process. And the taxpayers have to pay for it.

What do the social organizations and the National Rifle Association do? Instead of condemning the shooting and the manufacturers of the guns, they come out with a foolish argument that guns don't kill people, people kill people. This theory is not supported by majority of the police officers who have the job of upholding the law and order and in the process even die for it. They have all along maintained that guns, instead of protecting the victims, are more often responsible

for their deaths. But the NRA is the richest and the most powerful lobby in the Congress. It can easily sway the members of
concerned committees to win decisions in their favor.

The disgusting part of the whole issue is the people who
should be up in arms (sorry about the phrase!) against the
NRA lobby and those who support their theory are dancing
around the issue. Here is list of activities these people do
when a shooting at schools or public places occur: They offer
counseling services for parents and students, offer prayers on
school ground and in churches, form social networks, ask for
safety locks on guns, and insist on parents' accountability in
keeping the guns under lock and key and away from their
children, and so on. I call it dancing around the problem. In
fact, the American people do not want to get to the root of
the problem. They are against banning guns and rifles totally. They do not want to hold manufacturers of guns accountable for producing such weapons as the AK47. I am not
against those people who want to use guns for hunting purposes. Most countries around the world have made such pro-
visions. But most countries do not have the right to bear arms
in their national constitution, but their governments keep a
vigilant eye on the use of guns. They have created a different
culture to curb the activities of guns-related violence and
death. As a result, the percentage of gun-related deaths in
countries like the United Kingdom, Japan, and India is much
lower compared with that of the United States. After having
witnessed assassinations of U.S. presidents, public figures,
and other social activists, Americans still refuse to face the
reality that guns (not people) kill people. We can learn from
other countries. Shall we do it? I doubt it. Guns are a great
threat to our children and our liberty.

The Million Mom March in 2000 had raised high hopes
for the gun control. But it didn't help much in terms of impact
on our Congressmen. But in America we have to face political
realities. Gun control lobbies, like Handgun Control,

Coalition to Stop Gun Violence, and Violence Policy Center, have all realized that they have to compromise on the issue of gun control. I am with Rosie O' Donnell on the gun control problem. Politics is a game of compromise. That's what we have to do until we elect the politicians of our choice.

OUR CRISIS OF CONSCIENCE

❧

The other day I heard a sad news that a young student at the University of California at Berkeley refused to testify against a friend who had raped and shot an eight-year-old black child. This college was the setting for the incident, which occurred in the bathroom. The student refused to testify on the grounds that it was not his business and he was not getting involved in it. As is the case in such events, there is nothing the state or the university authorities can do to bring the perpetrator to justice or even just kick him out of the school.

What should the mother of the raped child do in such a situation? Being poor, she had no recourse to law. Those doors were closed for her. She appealed to the university authorities to take action against the student and kick out the unconscionable student from the school. Because the authorities expressed their inability on legal grounds, she started demonstrating on the Berkeley campus. She appealed to the conscience of the students and faculty members. Will it work? What may be legally justifiable is not always morally sound and socially acceptable. This was the focus of Rosa Parks when she refused to take a back seat on the public bus. By law, all blacks had to take a seat in the back. Only whites had the privilege to sit in the front. Rosa found Dr. King to air the grievance effectively. What was legally acceptable was morally reprehensible. Through boycott and political pressure, the wrong was righted. Is this mother of the murdered child expecting the same results?

Is this crisis of conscience new to American society? Is it confined to this country only? I think it's a deplorable, but it's a universal phenomenon.

In 1962 I read a shocking story of Kitty Genovese. As she was being stabbed to death, she was seen and heard by thirty-two people. Instead of calling the police or coming to her aid, they all closed their doors and windows! When asked by sociologists about their antisocial behavior, they told them that they didn't want to be involved. They were trying to protect their own families. What about the family of the young lady who was brutally stabbed right in front of their eyes? She had cried for help. Do we have any moral obligation to our society? Those who murder innocent people sometimes take the 5th Amendment and the witnesses to murders conveniently keep quiet on social issues that destroy innocent people.

OUR PRIORITY IN LIFE

⟋⟍

I do not like to watch TV with both eyes. It's boring. I prefer to watch it with one eye only while I am exercising or reading a book. But once in a while I do see a segment that brightens my day. I was watching an NBC channel, and there was an interview given by John Johnson, who was a TV anchorman on NBC's New York affiliate for many years. Before becoming an anchorman, he had covered many national and international events for NBC as a reporter. He was in the Desert War in the Middle East, right on the spot when the inmates in Attica Prison in New York revolted and took over the prison. Mr. Johnson had earned both fame and fortune, which few black men can claim it in this country.

It was mentioned in the interview that Johnson's father was a janitor at NBC in New York. His father wanted his son to go to college and get out of the den of poverty. Johnson covered the world events and circled the globe many times. But he had little time for his hard-working, aging father and his mother, who had cancer. After his mother's sudden death, Johnson had second look at the rat race he was engaged in. He made up his mind: He was going to give up his high-paying job as an anchorman. Just like that! He was going to spend the remainder of his life with his ailing father, playing with his two beautiful grandchildren, and take up painting again. Unfortunately, his father also died shortly.

"Did you ever regret?" the reporter asked him. Johnson answered, "Never. The only regret I have is that I didn't do it earlier."

What a magnificent resolution! In life, we have to put ourselves on the cross to experience the meaning and values in life. Buddha, Socrates, Christ, and many other great leaders have done it. You don't have to be a great leader to do it. But if you do it, you are on the path to greatness. Johnson is no small hero. He has shown through his example how all of us can change our lives by arranging priorities. It's not hard; it can be done with a stern resolution. The million dollar question is: Do you want to do it or stay in the rut until you die in it? You alone can make the difference in your life.

Think and act before it is too late!

THE DIVINE HAND

Sometimes you have to wonder why is it that you meet someone accidentally and somehow that person totally ruins your life. In the opposite direction, you might bump into somebody in a cafeteria or a shopping center by chance. You have never met him or her before, and your life is changed for the better on the information given by that individual.

This kind of situation has happened to me several times in my life. It makes me wonder: Is there such a thing as a "divine accident"? Is it planned by our destiny or the higher power that shapes our ends?

I also wonder if it is based on our past good or bad deeds, which the Hindus call the doctrine of Karma. I think in this life we enjoy good things or suffer on the basis of deeds in the past life. How else do you explain the birth of a child in Buckingham Palace in London or in the home of the Rockefeller family instead of in a slum in the streets of Calcutta? Consider this: In July 2002, some Russian teenagers were going for a vacation to Spain. They missed the morning flight and had to go by the noon flight. Unfortunately, the Russian plane by which they were traveling crashed because of technical failure. It was their first and the last vacation out of Russia.

Here is another coincidence: a lady rushes to the airport only to find that she was late by five minutes to catch her flight. She curses herself and the airline. After fifteen minutes driving back home on the highway, she hears on the radio that the flight she had missed had crashed ten minutes after the departure! She pulls the car at the curb and cries. How do we explain this miracle?

This thought of the divine hand has bothered me since my college days. I had a very brilliant college friend. He made straight A's in all his courses. He wrote poetry and plays. He was enrolled in engineering, made excellent grades in it, but after two semesters, he decided to be a medical doctor. In a year, he gave up that, too, and decided to major in languages. He excelled in that area as well.

Everyone knew he had a very bright academic future and was going to be a big shot. But destiny willed otherwise. At the age of twenty-eight, he died in a miserable way. For several years, he could not and did not tell any one that he was a victim of leprosy! No wonder in the hot Indian summer when we perspired, he wore long-sleeve shirts and a jacket. I thought he was crazy. After his sudden death, I learned that he was taking morphine shots at home! Before this horrible revelation, I used to tease him about marriage. "Why don't you get married and settle down? With your talents and financial background, any girl would love to be your life partner." He sighed and said, "Naren, how can I tell you? You will never understand the problems of others." How could I have known that he had leprosy? We were all shocked to know of it later. Why should my young friend die so young?

I wonder how come I continued to have good health and education in the United States and my friend died so young and was victimized by the ugly disease? How do you explain this human tragedy on the basis of reason alone? Is this divine justice? Does God know more about all of us than we do? Does He punish or reward human beings in this life on the basis of Karma? What we call injustice may not be so in His eyes because He knows more about human beings—their past and the future—than we as mortals do. He alone knows why more than 2800 men and women had to die in the World Trade Center twin towers in New York on September 11, 2001. Does it make any sense to you? But this is the only explanation I have to offer. Look into your own life, check out your own experiences, and you may agree with what the poet said: "It is the divinity that shapes our ends."

THE CLAMOR FOR A ROLE MODEL

A few years back, I visited a prison on the border of North Carolina and Virginia. One of my students was doing his internship there teaching prison inmates. Earlier I had visited women's prison in Raleigh, North Carolina, to find out how my students were doing there as teachers and mentors.

Visiting a prison is an unusual experience, like nothing else in one's life. It reminds you how lucky you are that *you* are not locked up inside those barbed wires and with no hope and no future. Except for the lack freedom and the special treatment they sometimes get at the hands of prison officers, prisons don't look like prisons. They have TV sets to watch, tennis and basketball courts to use, and library books to check out if they want. If they want to continue their education, the textbooks and teachers are provided with the compliments of taxpayers! I know from my own experience (as a visitor only) in India that not one similar type of facility is provided in Indian prisons (except books).

I was right in my observation to find that most of the inmates were blacks, perhaps because of the higher poverty level.

As a teacher I have believed in the philosophy of "open a school and close a prison." In America, our leaders believe in the anti-education philosophy of building more prisons, stricter punishments, longer sentences, and capital punishment as answers to crimes. As a teacher, I do not subscribe to that philosophy. I believe in educating the mind of a prisoner. Most of the prisoners do not want to be there. Sometimes, they rob banks and burglarize stores in their neighborhood because they do not have food and clothes for their families or have money to send their children to good schools. They and their children are condemned to the life of drudgery and misery. It is easy to pass judgment on them and conclude that they are no-good citizens. Conservatives tell us, "Lock them up and throw away the key." There may be some hardened criminals and drug dealers in prisons. It is not my intention to justify their antisocial behavior, but I am trying to understand them as a teacher.

My student teacher requested that I say a few words to his students. For the first time in life I was at a loss for words. What can I say to those unique students? The subject matter, the curriculum, the teaching methods I had learned, and the other learning tools I had sharpened over many years at the university were of no avail to me in this situation. Luckily, one of the students remarked during the session that if he had a role model to follow in life, he would not have landed in a prison like this. I noticed there was a big picture of Dr. Martin Luther King Jr. behind the man who made that remark. Earlier, the same prisoner had revealed to me that his mother had made a great sacrifice to put him through school. He had betrayed her trust.

I asked him what he thought of Dr. King as a role model for him to follow.

"Oh, man. That's a tall order to follow. I can't follow in his footsteps."

"Why not?" I persisted.

"I am not as big as he was."

"How about your own mom, who loved you so much and made sacrifices for you? Would you like to walk in her tiny shoes?" He didn't say a word and kept quiet for a long time.

The prisoner I met there represents thousands of men and women outside who might rationalize their behavior on the slippery ground that in this country there are no good role models to follow.

Start from your family, and then look outside. I always looked on my father as an excellent role model to follow. Many people who complain about the lack of good role models are looking for an excuse. There are role models in your homes, in your schools, in your churches and synagogues, and in larger society. I found them in India and in the United States also. What we lack is a strong will to follow in the shoes of the big fisherman. Many people love to talk about role models but don't want to take a chance to follow them in their own lives. Their behavior is inexcusable. Believe me, to follow a role model is indeed a tall order!

PERSPIRATION PAYS OFF RICH DIVIDENDS

If I am ever asked to give a single piece of advice to my son, I would immediately say: "Learn to work hard in your life. You can achieve anything. A lot of successful people have perspired to realize their goals. Follow their example."

I have seen in my family how the God-given talents have been wasted because they were plain lazy! They forgot the golden rule that even a diamond needs to be cut and rich land needs to be fertilized and cultivated. Lazy bones take you to your grave early!

I often see parents blaming their children for not imitating their neighbor's smart kid. We tend to forget that no two individuals are exactly alike. All children have some kind of talent, and parents should identify it and encourage the child and help him or her tap it. Instead, we compare our child with the neighbor's and degrade our own child. It's psychologically detrimental to the personality of the child. Parents should concentrate on the strength, not the weakness of their child. They should do everything to foster his or her interests. Having done it, they should emphasize the need for hard work. Interest plus hard work is the key to a child's success at school and in the larger world.

But our children also need a role model in a family. Parents need to create a learning climate in their family. If parents waste their time watching TV for hours and sleeping for the remaining time, they must not expect their children to be industrious and hard working. You have already set up a bad example for your kids.

When I was student at Madison, I shared an apartment with three other Indian students. I observed the study habits and academic performance of two friends majoring in pharmacology. These two students were friends and studied together back home in a college in Bombay. One was very shy but extremely intelligent, and the other was reasonably intelligent. The one with high level of intelligence worked less and made better grades compared with the other, who burned the midnight oil but couldn't compete with his friend academically. He was upset to see his friend listening to symphonies of Mozart and Beethoven and still making better grades. I have no way of knowing whether this student blamed God for making him less intelligent. But he had learned that God gives equal time to all human beings. It's up to us how to use it to our advantage. This student worked harder to compete with his classmate and made up for his lesser intelligence. He came close to beating him in class grades. Instead of cursing the Creator for making him less intelligent, he found a way around it and succeeded in his academic life. He was a shining example for many college students to follow. He showed what difference hard work makes in the academic life of a college student.

How many of our parents learn this lesson?

Hard work is the foundation of academic success and material prosperity in life.

THE BASIS OF OUR LOYALTY

When Aristotle taught in the Lyceum, one of his bright students started quoting Plato (who had taught Aristotle in the academy) to strengthen his argument. He did it three or four times. Aristotle neglected him in the beginning, but when the student persisted in his game, he bluntly told his arguing student, "Plato was great, but truth is greater!"

Artistotle taught us a great lesson in public and private life. It was he who taught us to think logically and not emotionally on issues in life. Unfortunately, we seldom take this approach. This is especially true when it comes to pledging our loyalty toward our friends and relatives. Our judgment is clouded by selfishness. We do not care whether we are doing the right thing or not. Our conscience (the divine radar) may tell us from within that what we are doing is wrong. But our self-interest takes a high priority over all other considerations.

Look at history. Richard Nixon, the late American president, wrote a book entitled *The Six Crises,* in which he discussed the place of loyalty in public life. He wanted his staff members to be loyal to him to the end, whether the leader (like him) was right or wrong. He didn't discuss any ethical problems involved in loyalty. This is an example of blind loyalty, which can be dangerous for an individual or a country.

This has been evoked by feudal kings and modern dictators. They have committed crimes against people and have asked their followers and servants to support them no matter what.

This raises a crucial question: should we support a leader, a dictator or, for that matter, a member of our own family, when we know that he or she is wrong? In most cases, we keep supporting these people, even though we know in our hearts that they are wrong. So why do we keep on doing the wrong thing? The obvious answer is our selfishness or the fear of punishment. We may be highly intelligent or greatly respectable in the public eye. But when it comes to self-interest, we set aside everything and the ethical principles take a back seat.

There is a beautiful story in Indian epic the *Mahabharat*. Draupadi, the wife of Pandavas, has been gambled away and lost to the enemies. They are out to undress her in public and humiliate her and her five husbands openly. In the court, there are great warrior counselors like Bhishma and Dronacharya who watch this ordeal with shame. When she implores them to intervene on her behalf, Bhishma, the leading authority on yoga and political wisdom, tells her, "My loyalty is to the king. I know what I am witnessing is wrong, but I can't help you!" This is a genuine human tragedy. We prefer not to help our relatives and friends in trouble even though they are on the right side! We become stark selfish or terribly afraid of the consequences.

There have been noble examples when leaders like Thomas à Beckett (not to mention Christ and Socrates) have stood up to kings and tyrants who were out to get them and destroy their conscience. Leaders expect their servants or followers to follow them blindly. This is the approach I call "My country, right or wrong." This unhealthy approach has ruined many countries, leaders, and people.

There comes a time in the life of an individual when he or she has to declare that he or she is no longer going to sit on the fence or support the wrong side. Enough is enough. That is what Rosa Parks did when she announced to the bus driver that she was tired of sitting in the back of the bus and that she was not going to leave her front seat! That would be a golden day for humanity when we take a bold stand and stand firm on principles and are willing to pay the price for it. We may become isolated or socially ostracized and shunned by our friends or relatives, but we can, at least, sleep in peace!

ROLE AND RELATIONSHIP

Some years back I explained to my son my theory of role and relationship in life. My main thesis was that our relationships change in life as we assume new roles in the family. When a person plays the role of a son, he has different relationship and responsibilities to carry out with the other family members. He is still playing a solo role. There are no serious commitments. There are differences of opinions but very little serious conflict. Making decisions is left to other elderly persons in the family.

But when the young man gets married and starts playing the new role of a husband, his whole relationship with his family changes. There is a new person, an outsider, in the family as an official new family member. Although a red carpet treatment is rolled out to her in the beginning, the carpet soon gets dusty and dirty and loses its original color when the power struggle between the daughter-in-law and the parents ensues. It creates an awkward position for the son. He can no longer afford to sit on a fence and watch the family conflict silently. The new tension is too much for him. He has got to take a side. And, in most cases, he stands behind his wife 100 percent whether she is right or wrong.

His silky relationship with his wife clouds his judgment. He forgets the years of sacrifice his parents made in his upbringing. They take a back seat. The role of a son has been replaced by the role of a husband, and it dominates his life. It takes a priority in his decision-making process. His wife, not his parents, come first. He will defend and take side of his wife whether she is right or wrong.

Why such a radical change in the attitude and behavior of a young man? Is it the marriage that has wrought this change? Or his role as a husband and consequently his behavior has changed? Does it happen to all newly-weds? Do they develop amnesia after their marriage that makes them forget the contributions made in the development of their lives?

This strange social phenomenon is sometimes nonetheless true. It is also true with girls. Their relationship with their own families (on the mother's side) also changes. Her husband and her children come first.

There is a great danger in the change of relationship because it makes you lose sight of objectivity in life. It makes you blind to the reality surrounding you. Sometimes you know that you are doing injustice to the opposite party. But love for your husband or wife prevents you from making the right decision.

If you try to be neutral most of the time, there is a danger of losing the backing of both sides. You are left alone. Your wife or mother will avoid you like the plague. Sitting on the fence doesn't help in a family situation.

I explained this theory to my son before he was about to get married. He assured me that it will never happen in his case. He would never leave his mother and will always serve her. My theory was put to test when he married a girl he was dating. Surprisingly, he did not tell his mother that he was married in a civil court. It came as a shock to her. He was her only son, and she had made tremendous sacrifice in bringing him up and educating him. I didn't know of his marriage for months because I was living in the United States. I had no problem with it, although I did not like his choice because his wife was not even a high school graduate. My wife condemned the marriage on the grounds that the girl had married her son for his money. A great change overcame my son. His marriage created a great distance between him and his mother, who never forgave him for marrying the wrong girl.

In this situation, my wife, being a very dominant person, made her son's life miserable. She kicked him and his wife from her home. Both of them were thrown on the street in the middle of the night. I had to come to their rescue. When I gave him money to find an apartment, my wife got mad. My relationship with her went from bad to worse. She told me that I had divided the family!

My son's marriage had totally changed his relationship with his mother and me. He told me later that my theory was sound and he had found it true from his experience. The same thing happened to my son that happens to millions of us when we start a new relationship in the family.

The other day, a guest lady talking on this issue remarked that after marriage girls tend to be closer to their parents. Is this true? I do not know. It depends how much freedom the girls enjoy after their marriage. Other factors, such as a husband's attitude toward his wife, the personality of the woman, the family structure, and roles played by family members. In this regard, I am reminded of an old Chinese saying: "Daughters are like water that splashes out of the family and cannot be gotten back after marriage." I do not know whether I agree with this maxim or not.

THE TEACHER: A HARD TASK-MASTER

I have always believed that a good teacher is worth a million dollars. But who is a good teacher? Here is my definition: A good teacher has the knowledge of Aristotle, conviction of Socrates, methodology of Anne Sullivan (the woman who taught Helen Keller), and love of Christ.

I am sure that most of our teachers do not meet all of the above criteria of a teacher. But after having taught for more than thirty-five years in India and the United States, I came to the conclusion that most of our teachers are not even hard task-masters. They put up with the poor performance of their students in the name of poverty, race, and fear of losing jobs or popularity. Teachers of all races are guilty of this terrible sin. Black teachers perhaps have a soft spot for the black students because of the color line, and white teachers may be trying to be nice because they do not want to feel guilty and be labeled as racists. They go easy on their students for reasons mentioned above. This is especially true with the teachers in teacher training colleges. In fact, they should be harder on their students and demand better quality and raise their expectations. We should remember that one bad teacher (like the one rotten apple spoiling the whole basket) can spoil the whole generation of students. We should exert great care in the selection standards, training, and evaluating our teachers. But this seldom happens.

Let us start with admission practices. Dr. J. B. Conant, the famous educator, in his book *The Education of American Teachers* (1964) recommended that the teacher training schools should select future teachers from the top 25 percent of their class. This is a great suggestion. In reality, the top students prefer not education but medicine, engineering, and business careers. Teaching is the choice of the lowest 25 percent of the students of the graduating high school class. Why? The obvious answer is money. If we can promise top salaries to top students, intelligent graduates will line up in large numbers in front of the teaching training colleges. This has not happened despite of recommendations from Dr. Conant, many commission reports on education, and teachers' organizations like the NEA and the AFT. American school boards want first-rate teachers with third-rate salaries. The school boards should first give them good salaries and then hold them accountable for their poor performance.

Second, take the case of admission standards for teachers. To get students, some schools lower their standards. What kind of performance can you expect from such students?

Finally, a word about the teachers who train such students. Most teachers, in my observation, instead of raising the expectations of their students, go to the level of their students in the name of understanding. I am not against understanding the socioeconomic background of their students. But we should motivate them, raise their expectations, and demand high levels of performance despite their family background.

The Pygmalion in the Classroom is a study that should be made mandatory reading for all teachers. Unfortunately, most of our teachers read very little. We had ordered more than twenty-five copies of *Pygmalion* in the classroom. Very few of our teachers read the book. The few that had hardly mentioned it during class discussions. Our teachers are poor readers and are poorly grounded in the subject matter.

They do not read on their own nor are they mandated to read by the teachers in the teacher training colleges. Many teachers at training colleges are only textbook teachers. What can you expect from such teachers? You have to have an academic level to raise the expectations of your students. Once these teachers get their doctorates, they bid good-bye to more reading and learning.

Another great tragedy of the teacher training program is the period that is allotted for field experience. The time given for teachers is, most of the time, only three months. During that period, the teacher under training works under the supervision of a local schoolteacher called a cooperative teacher. First, this internship period is too short to get a real feel for the classroom situation they have to face later. The supervising teacher from the college has too many students to supervise. It's difficult for him or her to pay special attention to the students. Very few have follow-up sessions with their supervised students. No wonder many teachers often quit the job before they start their teaching. To make the situation worse, the college instructors who teach theory of education, educational psychology, and teaching methods are out of touch with the reality in public schools. They have doctorates or advanced degrees, but they very seldom take courses to update their education. They live in their ivory towers and lecture on courses as scheduled.

What can you expect from such teachers under training and from those who train them? How do you find good teachers who measure up to our standards and do a great job in the classroom? Money alone will not help. The incentive will have to come from some other quarters. Marva Collins, the successful Chicago schoolteacher, not only found students but also motivated them to read classics in elementary schools!

The teacher training colleges can learn from her experience. No wonder the teacher training colleges are in deep trouble. They need to be overhauled now.

THE ROLE OF THE MEDIA

I have visited many countries in the Middle East as well as Asian counties. I have stayed in the United States and watched the print and the electronic media for years. I am getting more convinced that there is no such thing as 100 percent free press. In the dictatorial countries like China, Cuba, and North Korea, the question of free media does not exist. They are all under one control, that of the state. But this is not so in democratic countries. The media is supposed to be totally free if not fair all the time. We print everything that is fit to print.

During the British colonial days in India, the government obviously controlled the media so that they could rule India from London. When India earned independence in 1947, I thought the media would be in the hands of Indians and it would be the ultimate voice of the people. I was terribly disillusioned. In free India, the press was ruled by Indians who had the means and resources to control it. There was only a change of guard. The inside people remained the same—the rich and the super-rich. The capitalists rule the Indian media. This is not true in just Asian and Latin American countries, but all over the world, including America.

The freedom of the press guaranteed by the U.S. Constitution remains intact on paper. If our print and the electronic media are not free, then the question arises as to who owns it. The answer is the big corporations in all countries. They, not the editors or the prominent newscasters on TV, are calling the shots.

Liberals blame the capitalists for controlling the media and right-wingers jump on the media for the left bias. Both blame Washington lobbyists and corporations for influencing the media as well as the politics of this country. There is no end to this blame game.

There is no question in my mind (I am sure it is also in the minds of millions like me) that during the past twenty years, the media has lost a lot of its freedom to the big corporations. All you have to do is to take a close look at the ownership of our major TV networks. General Electric ($1299 billion in revenues) controls NBC and all its affiliate networks. Similarly, Disney ($25.4 billion) owns ABC, the Disney Channel, and others. Viacom ($20 billion) is in control of CBS and its affiliates. In a situation like this, can Rupert Murdoch be left behind? No way! He owns Fox and its affiliates.

Fearful as it may sound, these companies are expanding their financial empire into other lucrative areas, such as the music and magazine industries. Where does it stop? This is all being done in the name of free enterprise and globalization! Big companies are gobbling up small companies, and millions of employees are being laid off all in the name of saving money and to please stockholders. What is the place for a small person in these big corporations when big fish gobble up small fish? He is invisible.

Under these circumstances, how can the media be free and frank? Big companies like G.E. and Enron have been heavily fined by the federal, state, and some local governments for violating laws. The tall claim of G.E., "We bring good things to life" sounds hollow. These big corporations have lobbyists working for them and have succeeded tremendously in keeping the members of both political parties in their pockets. Because the bottom line for them is profits, they will do anything and use all powers to suppress the truth in the media and fire anybody who challenges their authority. People have started organizing all over the world to fight these big corporations, but they have limited resources, making their struggle very difficult.

I don't like total control of the media in the hands of the State like in China, but what we have in America is no better than the communist system except our TV anchormen and -women are getting fat salaries but very little professional freedom. This situation reminds me of the old saying, "One is dead and the other is yet unborn." What should we do now?

ATTRACTING THE BEST TEACHERS

Some years back, I wrote a poem to draw public attention to the humiliating salaries of public school teachers in America.

I would rather
be a plumber to
to fix a leaking bathroom
than be a teacher
to labor for five dollars an hour
and beat my brains
in a classroom.

When I wrote those lines, I had called a plumber a week before to get the leak in my bathroom fixed. It being a Saturday, he told me in advance on phone that I will have to pay him overtime charge. His charge was $30 an hour or fraction of it. He was only a high school graduate and was making more money per hour than a man like me with a doctorate.

I come from a teaching family in India. My grandfather was a teacher and so was my father. He taught for thirty years in public school in India and retired on pension of 95 rupees (approximately $3) a month. He had a hard time making ends meet. He worked from five in the morning until he went to bed. He was bitter as a teacher and was very critical about the teacher salaries in India. He never wanted to be a teacher, but his father had forced him into teaching. It added to his frustration. He told me that he didn't want anyone in his family to be a teacher.

I graduated with an honor's degree in education and languages and had a teaching certificate to practice teaching. When I told my father that I had decided to become a teacher and help society, he told me, "Naren, be a beggar and sit near a temple. You will earn more money than a teacher earns in a classroom." I knew he meant every word of it. He was fed up with teaching and the salary associated with it. But I was not going to change my profession because there was no money in teaching. I looked on teaching as a social instrument to change society. That was my motivation.

When I taught in North Carolina at one of the state universities, one of my graduate students (when he was about to take his final examination at the end of the semester) wrote me an eye-opening letter explaining why he had decided to skip the semester exam. In his letter he had written,

> *Dear Dr. Tambe,*
>
> *I came to see you earlier in you office. Sorry, I missed you. I have taken up a job at local post office. My starting salary will be $33,000 compared with $19,000 at a private school as an assistant principal. Needless to say I will not be returning to take the final exam and be a teacher later. I thoroughly enjoyed your classes in principalship. You motivated me. But considering the salary and the prevailing classroom situation, I have decided to quit teaching in favor of post office job. There is less stress and more money.*

Like my father's advice, this letter forced me to take another look at the teaching profession As an educator, I now realize that low teaching salaries is a worldwide phenomenon. We cannot attract first-rate teachers with third-rate salaries. Teachers all over the world have a fundamental right to a decent and a compatible salary.

Many years ago, Dr. J. B. Conant, the leading educator of his time, recommended that the teachers should be selected from the top 25 percent of a graduating class. How can the quality of public education improve with the help of such teachers who become teaches as a last resort? Most of them come from the bottom of their classes. No wonder in 2002, our Education Secretary Rod Paige, in his report to Congress gave the teachers a big F. Those who are on the top of their classes become doctors, engineers, and attorneys. They know there is neither money nor prestige in teaching. Why should they beat their brains against the four walls of a classroom?

This shameful situation has to change. I am fully aware of the need for performance and accountability on the part of teachers. But first let them have competitive salaries and a voice in the decision-making process and *then* hold them accountable. You can't expect an elephant to dance all day by feeding him a small bag of peanuts!

In a society where human beings are judged not by their values but by new cars and big houses, bank balances and fashionable clothes, we have to provide our teachers with good salaries and then hold them accountable. If we don't do something in time to help teachers, they will soon be plumbers and start clearing choked-up drains and earn more money rather than try in vain to control the unruly children in the classroom and earn less. Can you blame them for their decision?

We need excellent teachers but American society should get ready to pay the price for it. If we can offer higher salaries to our sports coaches, we can also offer better salaries to our teachers who shape the future of our children.

HIDING BEHIND THE SHIELD OF POVERTY

When I taught education at a predominately African American college, I noticed two things: most of our students were poor and were either on state-funded scholarships or doing part-time jobs to meet their college expenses. Second, I observed that the majority of our students had become fatalists. I found them hiding behind the shield of poverty. Some of them who came to my office for guidance or recommendation had given up on society and as such, they didn't want to work hard because they had a preconceived ideas that the white society was not going to help them win the war on poverty.

I argued with them by giving shining examples from the lives of James Baldwin, Sidney Poitier, Whitney Houston, and Michael Jordan. It didn't work. They were not interested in hard work but were looking for a scapegoat.

When I was a student at the University of Oklahoma, I had an Italian psychology teacher. On his office door, he had written in bold words, "Poverty causes some to break, others to break their records." I quoted this saying to my students many times, but it had very little effect on them. Most of them told me, "It's fine, but it's not going to work in my case." They had lost faith in themselves. It was drummed into their heads for years that they were no good. It was an experiment in brainwashing, and the white power structure in the South had succeeded in doing the job effectively.

Although my students understood the game, they didn't want to fight it. They had lost their will to stand up and accept the social challenge. The examples of Rosa Parks and Dr. Martin Luther King Jr. did not help them.

I also realized that I couldn't do the job of helping such students alone. I needed help from their parents. I had a few conferences with some parents. They showed interest in my idea but told me that they had no control over their grown-up kids!

I have no sympathy for lazy loafers in schools. They come to school to while away their time. They distract the attention of some good and promising students. It is very difficult to separate good students from trouble-makers. Unfortunately, the teacher has very little authority in a public school to kick them out. Students have threatened them, and some teachers have lost their lives. How does a teacher like me inspire some promising students and put them on the promising track?

I learn that as a teacher, you do the best you can to help students. The rest is up to them. Poverty is not a crime, but hiding behind the shield of poverty is a first-rate crime. It should not be encouraged.

NOT IQ, BUT I WILL

One of the saddest things I have observed among students is the lack of strong will and personal commitment to learning. According to the latest educational fad, a teacher is described as a facilitator. He or she is supposed to facilitate the process of learning for students. How in the world can one facilitate the process of learning if a student does not have the will or has no commitment to learning?

I have yet to see a teacher who has shown his or her students the art of developing a strong will power and get a commitment to learning. First, developing a strong will in a student is a long-term process. In addition, it needs a teacher's commitment to the students. A teacher has to establish the bond with the students to win their trust. Through his or her own example, the teacher has to show and encourage students how to develop a strong will to learn. If a teacher does not love the students like his or her own children, the task of encouraging and developing a strong will becomes more difficult. Love creates a strong bond between the two and strengths commitment to learning. It's no small task and it needs patience.

Unfortunately, in public schools, strong will and a good commitment are in short supply. A number of reasons—such as the quality of teacher hired, increased teaching load, crowded classrooms, and the lack of academic freedom—could be listed as some problems that leave little room to maneuver students in the direction of will development and sharpen their commitment to learning.

The teacher also needs to be taught a course in these two arts at the teacher training colleges so that when they become full-fledged teachers they can test their skills and help their students develop these two skills. Unfortunately our teacher training colleges teach courses in theory and methodology which have very little bearing on the realities in public or private schools. No wonder these training colleges are losing ground and have become targets of criticism of educators and the general public. The old saying, "Where there is will, there is a way" is half true. Simply believing in a will never shows the way or direction to our students. A strong will needs to be rooted in our children at an early age by their parents, and teachers should build on it later. If this is done, perhaps up to 50 percent of our students' failure could be eliminated. As of today, for lack of strong will and commitment to learning, our students look like flat tires in schools. Students need to be shaken up, and the method for teacher training must be overhauled and oiled with a new vision.

History is full of examples of ordinary people becoming extraordinary heroes through sheer will and commitment to a cause. They were not geniuses but were ordinary men and women like you and me. Abraham Lincoln and Mahatma Gandhi are two outstanding examples. They were common people, but they had uncommonly strong will and unusual commitment to their causes. These leaders had failed many a time in public life, but they never gave up. They kept on going despite all odds. Finally, they succeeded in their goals.

If Lincoln and Gandhi can do it, so can our student in schools whose job looks minuscule compared with gigantic tasks these two great leaders undertook and finished. Our teachers should use such shining examples from the lives of great men and women to inspire their students and strengthen their will to succeed in school life.

On this subject, I would strongly urge readers and teachers to read an excellent autobiography written by Sammy Davis Jr., the famous singer. His is a modern story of a man's strong will and commitment to music.

RELIGION: THE OPIATE OF THE MASSES

Karl Marx wrote that religion is the opiate of the masses. As a sociologist, he understood very well the role of religion in a bourgeois society. Marx was partly right when he wrote it. What he was trying to convey that in the Western democratic culture of the time, the religious leaders, in collaboration with other powerful agencies, had used religion to keep people ignorant so that they could be exploited. The religious leaders used the religious "opiate" to sooth and quiet the people to distract their attention from important social and economic issues. Under the hypnotic power of religion the thinking capacity of the members is paralyzed. They become numb and blind to the social realities that surround them. They accept without question the authority of their religious leaders and support the social power structure.

What Marx was trying to convey was that by using religion as opiate, people could be brainwashed. If we start analyzing the messages of our religious leaders like Jimmy Swaggart, Jim Bakker,, Pat Robertson, the late Ayatollah Khomeini, and many others preaching on TV, we become convinced that these men have used religion and openly cheated their ignorant followers out of their millions of dollars only to build their own wealthy empire.

Also consider the government as an ally of these religious leaders. As a team they have taken advantage in exploiting ignorant people for centuries. During the regime of Peter the Great in Russia, the church and the state joined hands to maintain slavery and serfdom . The pope did it in England centuries ago and still continues to use his scepter to punish people in Latin America; mullahs have done it in the Muslim society, including Pakistan, and the Hindu priests do the same in predominantly Hindu India. This has been their consistent pattern in the history of the world. Under these conditions, not only the poor suffered but also great scientists and thinkers like Galileo, Copernicus, and many others suffered in the past. Even today literary giants like Salman Rushdie and Bangladeshi Taslima Nasreen become victims of the wrath of Christian and Muslim religious fanatics.

Marx was a serious student of history and his conclusion that religion had played a reactionary role in world history should be understood in this context. A lot of blood has been shed in the name of religion. According to one study, 96 percent of the world's wars and battles have been fought in the name of religion. The Dark Ages and the Crusades are excellent proof of this. We still go on killing people in India, Ireland, Algeria, and the Middle East, all in the name of holy war! When is it going to stop?

The framers of the American constitution and Karl Marx were not against religion, but they were dead set against religious practices that burned people as witches. So James Madison and Thomas Jefferson inserted the first amendment to keep government and religion separate and at the same time ensuring the right of every American to follow his or her faith without any fear or favor or retribution. I think Marx might well have appreciated first amendment very much Unlike Marx, the founding fathers understood very well the power and role of religion in the lives of the people in all walks of life. They didn't ban religion entirely (except in public schools);

communist countries like China, the former Soviet Union, and Cuba banned religion in schools. History proves that the American founding fathers were right and the leaders of the communist countries were wrong.

Religion serves as an elixir if used wisely to meet spiritual needs of the people. But if religion is used unwisely, history tells us it can also act like dynamite to destroy lives. The founding fathers and the framers of the U.S. Constitution had drawn a line between religion and religious fanaticism. The First Amendment is a real tribute to the foresight of our founding fathers and a permanent warning to religious fanatics all over the world.

LOVE, PREJUDICE, AND FAMILY

A few years back, I was invited to the birthday party of my friend's granddaughter. I went there with a gift for the young lady who was six years old. She was about to be enrolled in elementary school. I knew the girl's mother very well. She had not bothered to show up on her daughter's birthday! It didn't come as a surprise to me. When I gave her my birthday gift and was about to kiss the girl on her cheek, she turned her face away and said, "I don't like to be kissed by a black man." Obviously, she could not distinguish between black and brown.

Being a friend of the family for many years, her grand-mother immediately scolded her. It was too late. I was not insulted, but I felt sorry for the child for having a prejudiced grandmother who had done a poor job of educating the child. I don't blame the child for her prejudiced behavior. In fact, she didn't understand the meaning of the word *prejudice*. But I certainly blame the parents of such a child.

My educated guess was that her parents must be talking about the blacks and browns like me not favorably at home, and the child must have picked up the information automat-ically at the dinning table or in the living room. I have known her grandmother for years. She has a small business and does very well. She is not even a high school graduate. I know that she is terribly prejudiced against blacks. When I go to eat at her place, I have seen three or four black girls working for her in the kitchen. That doesn't stop her hating them. The black folks help her make money, but she has no social contacts with them.

One time, I went to her church to see the company she keeps on Sundays. She is a devoted Christian. But like many people in this country, she and her church-going friends have been practicing discrimination inside and outside their church. Just like some international club members who pledge allegiance to the American flag and believe in one nation under God with liberty and justice for all yet in their own clubs do not allow any blacks or other minorities to join or attend! All the members of my friend's congregation were white. I was the sole exception because I was brown (not a black) and an invited guest!

When the girl refused a kiss on her cheek from me, I was not insulted. I blamed her parents for giving this child such a prejudiced mind. As a teacher I have always believed "Show me a decent child and I will show you a decent family." Our children are not born with prejudice, preferences, or love. When the child is born in the hospital, the child doesn't should at birth "I hate you, I hate you.." The child's mind at birth, as Locke stated, is a clean slate. We write prejudices or love on this slate. It's the planting of our parents that speak loudly in later years. They become the carriers of our prejudices and preferences. As parents we should always remember that prejudiced and broken minds do more harm to a child than broken homes and broken families. It is not essential to leave millions of dollars, a beautiful home, or stocks and bonds for your children in your will. The most precious gift parents can leave behind for their children is the gift of a clean mind and the gift of love. This great gift will not only enrich the lives of your children alone but will also nourish their souls.

CHRIST AND SOCRATES

During my college days in India and the United States, I was greatly under the influence of Socrates. I read a lot on him. As is well known, what the world knows about this great man and scholar is from his famous disciple, Plato. The information on him, his views politics, ethics, literature, and life are compiled by Plato in his famous book *The Republic*. On this book, Emerson commented, "Burn on the books in all the libraries for their value is in one book: *The Republic*." Of course, this was an exaggeration. Socrates wrote no book, so we have to rely on Plato and his interpretation of his master's views.

When Socrates was put to death, Plato was a young man of twenty-eight years. It should not come as a surprise that his views on his dear master were colored. In his book, he does not say one word about Socrates to harm his reputation. To Plato, Socrates was an infallible hero. He worshiped the ground Socrates walked on.

There is no question that Socrates, the son of an ordinary stone cutter, was highly intelligent. He was a seeker of truth. He asked questions to many professionals and exposed them as "know-nothings." When people asked for answers from Socrates, he openly confessed that all he knew was that he knew nothing!

As an intellectual giant, Socrates appealed to the head through his method of questioning and reasoning. He was dispassionate and analytical in his arguments. There was no room for emotions. It seems that he took great delight in exposing the pundits of Athens. As a result, he made many enemies. They ganged up against him at the time of his trial and played an important role in his execution. We learn from Plato's account that Socrates took the deadly poison hemlock serenely and ended his life peacefully. He is reported to have remarked that he preferred to die so that truth may live! A noble life ended with a violent death!

And now about Christ.

There are some similarities between Christ and Socrates. Both had great faith in what they were doing and were highly committed to the spiritual welfare of their followers. Both showed tremendous moral courage when they were faced with death. They were searching for eternal and permanent values that enrich the lives of human beings. Both met violent death.

But the important difference lay in the pursuit of their objectives. Socrates used reason and logical method to extricate truth out of the people he questioned. He was merciless in his approach and did not hesitate to expose the ignorance of his questioners. He must have received great satisfaction in doing so. But he certainly rubbed the people the wrong way. And they did not forget it. At the time of his trial, they took their final revenge on him and got rid of him forever! The man who was trying to save their souls lost his life because his method was not accepted.

Unlike Socrates, Christ appealed not to the heads but to the hearts of his followers. As a religious leader, he knew too well that in life people are more emotional than rational and that he had to change his method of teaching.

He used the power of love to teach and touch the lives of millions. His background as a preacher helped him use the language with great skill, and he used it effectively to carry on his divine message. Christ was one of the greatest and most effective communicators of the world. His sermon on the mount is a prime example.

These men were two great servants of humankind. Both were advocates of spiritual values. What can we learn from their lives? First, to succeed in public life, rely more on emotion and less on reason to realize your objectives. If you use only cold logic, your message may be confined to the four walls of the academic world only. If you want a wider audience, appeal to people's hearts. Try love. Second, even though sometimes people are wrong, chide them in a gentle manner in private. Don't expose them in public. It humiliates them. It fosters animosity and encourages among them the tendency to get even with you later.

Is it a guarantee that if you use love, your life is secured? Not at all. Look at the life of Christ again. He was crucified! Was it because he berated the money-lenders doing business in the temple? There is no question about it. How else do you explain the behavior of the mad crowd when it was given the choice by the governor to choose between Christ and a criminal? They chose Barabbas over Christ. The money-lenders had not forgotten the public humiliation and the man who threatened their profits! They led the mob that called for his crucifixion and put Christ on the cross. Today, nobody remembers the names of people who voted for the deaths of Christ and Socrates. One thing is certain. Christ has a wider appeal to humankind because of his method. Love conquers all. It is a better method.

SILENCE IS GOLDEN AND CREATIVE

Is there any strength in silence? Is it spiritual or practical? I was curious to find out about the mystery of silence.

When I was in India I had a college teacher who observed silence once a month. I had also read about Gandhi's many experiments with truth, one of which was his weekly practice of observing silence every Monday. He didn't speak. He wrote on a slate to communicate with the people who came to see him and discussed political or personal problems. Then there was my master, living in a jungle in a small village in India. He did not talk for six days each week! Only on Sunday did he mingle and talk to the people who came to see and pay their respects to him. There was also one of the greatest spiritual leaders of modern India, Shri Aurbindo. He lived in Pondichery, a former French colony in India. He totally cut himself off from the world and came out of his abode only three times a year to greet the people. He also experimented with silence and immortality.

How does silence help us grow as human beings? Are we talking too much and wasting our creative energy? Are our senses affected or benumbed by external forces, such TV, radio, reading, or listening to people? There is no question about it that especially TV and the music industry have somewhat deafened us to other things! We don't have time to communicate with our family members or our neighbors. We are under the complete control of that mad, mad box. Our eyes and our children's eyes are glued to TV sets. This situation has reached a crisis. We do not have time to think. We religiously believe as the gospel truth what media commentators tell us every morning and evening. We don't have time nor do we want to check out their so-called facts.

Apart from information, the media pour advertisements into our ears and eyes. The worst part of it is that we are not left alone by them. For that, *we* (not the media) are responsible. We *allow* the media to dominate our mental faculties. We always have an option to turn off our TV sets. If the government tomorrow decides to ban TV or regulate TV hours, Americans will be up in arms!

I am beginning to see the dark side of media saturation. It destroys not only human relations but also hampers creativity. As a student in this country, I didn't have money to buy a TV set. I spent more time reading in the library and meeting my friends. My life soon changed when I got a job and when I bought a TV set. My writing and reading took a back seat. It took me many years to get rid of this addiction. Now I have become a selective TV watcher. I watch the evening news and selective programs on educational channel. I used to have cable, but I discontinued it. There were some good educational programs on the Learning Channel, the Disney Channel, and Nickelodeon, but they were few and far between. Most of the programs were violent, sexy, and unfit for adults or children to watch at any time.

My big quarrel with the print and the electronic media is that they destroy creativity. They are real obstacles in the development of your creativity. When you watch TV, listen to music, or read a newspaper, your mind is not necessarily stimulated. Your creative energy is stifled inside. There is no room for new ideas to enter. Just like the poet said, "We have eyes that see not and ears that hear not / we have given our hearts away." This is a real tragedy. Is it just an American tragedy? No. In this global and technological revolution, it has become a global tragedy. I see Indian children in India glued to children with the blessings of their parents.

Silence is the language of Gods. If we want to get in touch with God and also with our inner soul, silence is the medium we have to use to unlock the hidden treasure. How can you do it? Just walk in the woods alone and listen to the birds or the whispering winds that slowly creep through the leaves of trees. Listen quietly to the silent songs of flowing streams. Or work in the garden for a few hours. Just be natural in the world and feel yourself in unity with nature. How peaceful it is to be in the company of silent servants of God! Do you now feel the nearness or the existence of God? If not now, through practice of silence you will soon feel it. Release your creative potentials and realize your inner strength.

Silence is the key . Start observing silence one day a week and then slowly increase it. You will see a gradual change in your attitude and behavior. Silence will open the door to inner peace. If you are an artist, you will see creativity flowing from within. Remember: Silence is not only golden but also creative.

SOME ARE MORE EQUAL THAN OTHERS

According to many polls taken recently, American people believe that the most important question the country has to pay attention to and fix it is education. In the 2000 general elections, the number one issue was again education. Unfortunately, the leaders of both political parties are paying only lip service to education. They know too well the problems, but they don't want to face the issue head on.

The problem of education is bad in America, but it is the worst in case of the education of the black. Our politicians, education pundits, and scholars have occasionally criticized historically African American state colleges and universities. Some Harvard scholars have studied such colleges and have condemned them as "pockets of academic disaster." A few of them have openly suggested that instead of wasting money on them, they be closed!

Unfortunately, their message is trickling down into the heads of our state legislators and they have started to consolidate these colleges and have come out with devices to cut off their programs and funding to put them out of business. There used to be more than 123 black colleges and universities in the United States, most of which are located in the South. That number has considerably decreased. Black folks have done a tremendous job of supporting these colleges (public and private) financially. If they had not done so, millions of minority students today would be without education and basic skills.

Sociologists like David Riesman criticize these black schools on the ground that they have no educational quality. What good is it to criticize a poor man for lack of good dress when he has no food for his stomach? What these people do not understand is the fact that the current top priority of black colleges is their survival and continued existence, not necessarily the quality of education. Empty stomachs do not care either for quality or morality. It's idle talk about them. Only arm-chair scholars like Riesman can wag their tongues about it and get paid to do so! What is true about black schools is equally true about Native American schools as well as the schools run by and for Hispanics.

What these minority colleges badly need is vitamin M—*money.* Hold them accountable, but for God's sake, don't starve them to death. Give them enough money first and then hold them accountable after some years. Just like when you plant, fertilize, and water an apple tree, you do not get fruit overnight. It takes years to see a crop. The same is the case with minority colleges. These people have been neglected for years and often denied access to education. How can they learn or acquire skills instantly? It is going to take a lot of training and patience to get results.

We do not realize that in the name of free enterprise, we have perpetuated a segregated funding system for these colleges. In more than twenty-five states, the state supreme courts have declared state funding of public schools unconstitutional. The U.S. Supreme Court in its 1982 *Rodriguez v. State of Texas* historical decision also criticized this unequal funding method of public schools but would not rule it unconstitutional because, according to U.S. constitution, there is no *right* to education! What a nice technical loophole they found!

But I am not concerned with the legal side of funding public schools or state colleges. I am worried about the moral side. Do we realize that by unequal funding and discriminating against blacks and other minority schools, we the people are the losers? We lose money, we lose face in the eyes of the world, and we create resentment among minority students. We sow the seeds of hostility ourselves.

Look at the private funding patterns for white and black schools. In my city of Durham, North Carolina, some philanthropists and Research Triangle Park industries have given donations of up to a million dollars to private high schools and predominately white schools! They have rarely shown such generosity to black or minority colleges. Are blacks not equal taxpayers? Why shouldn't they refuse to pay their taxes for white schools when their own children denied equal funding? No equal taxation unless they get equal education for their children—is it not a sound principle of taxation? Did not the Americans fight the colonial British powers for the same principle?

The radio ad urging us to give the college of our choice makes little sense to me because white donors give mainly to white schools, colleges, and universities and throw crumbs only at black colleges. One time I saw the picture of the president of an industry and the chancellor of a local black university in a newspaper because the industry had donated $3,000 to the black college! I thought the industry's generosity knew no bounds!

I am not a socialist or a communist. But this method, all in the name of free enterprise, is one of the worst aspects of the capitalist system I have ever seen. The state is equal guilty of the same crime. North Carolina had enough money to run a model high school known as North Carolina School of Science and Math. I am not against the existence of this school; it has done a great job. But I resent the fact that it is possibly done at the cost of black colleges in North Carolina.

The courts have also criticized the funding system of white and black colleges in many Southern states. I know the educational systems in Russia and China have professed equality to the public, yet have systematically promoted the concept of "some are more equal than others."

Our constitution proclaims equality, and our educators are never tired of hammering on the theme of equality of educational opportunities. In reality, the picture is totally different. We hate communism but still love to practice their ideology in education. It's an American tragedy. I see an ugly face of free enterprise in this educational practice of funding, which makes rich schools richer and the poor schools poorer. It has to stop.

THE JOY OF SELFLESS GIVING

In the Hindu holy book, *The Bhagavad Gita,* there is one important verse that is my favorite. It translates like this: To work, you have the right but not to the fruits thereof. What it actually means is that do your duty in life toward your family, society, or country. But you may not expect anything in return. If you expect anything as a reward, you sow the seeds of unhappiness. I didn't realize its meaning until I experienced its practical effect in my life.

I was very young and ideal. I wanted to change society based on socialist ideals. I read Plato's works, books by A. S. Neil, Pestaolozzi, Froebel, and Montessori and discussed how their ideas could be translated into schools. My classmates and I worked very hard.

As a socialist in India, I couldn't get a job in any school because the then ruling party did not like socialists or communists and most of the school owners subscribed to that ideology to secure some benefits from the government. Against all financial odds, some of our like-minded socialists started an elementary/secondary school. To put our ideals to test through education, we were going to change Indian society in our city.

We didn't have any money. We could not pay our teachers! We didn't have a building to house our students. We turned an old, government -owned warehouse into a school.

The iron sheets used as roofs in the warehouse made our lives miserable. In summer the temperature shot beyond 100°F, and we had to go out and hold classes under the tree to cool off. Neither our students nor their parents complained about our unusual location. They knew that we loved our students and we would teach under any physical conditions. The parents supported us educationally and financially. They were extremely generous. All of us, teachers and school administrators, lived up to the parents' educational expectations.

We always had a problem with money. Many school principals and their managers in our city made every effort to defame us. Some brought pressure on the government with a petition not to recognize our school. It made harder for us to go out and collect donations from school patrons and donors. First, we were socialists. We had declared war on capitalists, who had all the money. But it was our policy never to practice politics within the four walls of the school. We were free do anything when the school was out and outside the school premises. Our teachers knew the rules of the game.

As I look back, I felt so good doing something for the society without expecting any reward. I was doing the job as a duty and paying off my debt to society.

I am not a socialist anymore. I am not impressed with our so-called capitalism and free enterprise either. There are many holes in this system. We touched the lives of many youngsters, some of whom have settled in America as doctors, engineers, and businessmen. I often get phone calls from them, and some visit me to express their gratitude. I feel rewarded. One student touched my feet when I was coming out the post office in India to show his respect. He said, "Mr. Tambe, I meet you after so many years. You gave me admission and scholarship and encouraged me. It paid off. I am now an engineer. I want to thank you for what you did for me when I needed all the help. My mother was a widow when you gave me admission at your school. Sir, thank you so much for the timely help. I will always remember it." I didn't remember his name and had forgotten his face. But he remembered everything that I had done for him. I was so glad it worked out for him. How do I measure our success in a case like this?

I did my duty. I didn't expect anything from anybody. But the divine laws have the tendency to work in their own way.

What did I learn from my experience? First, there is always an inner satisfaction when you do something for society as your duty and without expecting any reward. Your services may not be measured in terms of money. Don't be surprised if your efforts are not ever recognized and rewarded by the society. Just as Robert Browning expressed in his immortal poem "The Patriot," "Oh God, I have done my duty, it is up to you to answer for your actions."

Second, there is a great misconception that only money can truly motivate human beings. This is wrong. Take a good look at world history. Great tasks have been accomplished not by money but through the selfless commitments of individuals to a great cause. Marie Curie of France, who won the Nobel Prize in chemistry, injected herself to find out the effects of radium. Sometimes, a nonmonetary element can motivate you greatly. Gandhi was asked what kept him going in his old age and despite the frustrations surrounding him. He reportedly remarked that every time he felt isolated and dejected, he brought before his mind's eye the face of the poorest of the poor in India and his battery was recharged. Thousands of missionaries working in Africa and Asia to relieve the suffering of the poor are motivated not by dollars but by love of Christ. Father Defian lived among the lepers in Hawaii to serve them and contracted leprosy himself. What motivated him except love of Christ? It's high time the managers of motivation and advocates of the gospel of greed had a good look at this other aspect of the life of human beings which is also a powerful factor in motivation. Love and selfless giving for the good of society also count!

GANDHI'S INFLUENCE ON DR. MARTIN LUTHER KING JR.

Mahatma Gandhi of India and Dr. Martin Luther King Jr. of the United States were the two of the most outstanding and unique leaders of the twentieth century. Both of them were assassinated by fanatics who spread the poison of hate. Gandhi and King not only changed the course of politics in their countries but also influenced the methods of solving social and political problems. The impact of their philosophy and their influence is still in evidence all over the world, especially in developing countries in Africa and Asia. Nelson Mandela of South Africa openly acknowledged his political debt to Gandhi and his nonviolent approach to the solution of their problems.

It is well known that Gandhi and Dr. King never met (King was still a teenager when Gandhi was assassinated), but Gandhi was so frustrated with his own followers and prevailing conditions then in India that, like a prophet, he wrote in his diary that his philosophy of nonviolence someday would be manifested by a Negro in the world. Dr. King had read the works of Gandhi and had digested his nonviolent methods of solving political problems thoroughly. But he was not sure about the efficacy and effectiveness of some of Gandhi's methods, such as fasting.

Despite their divergent religious backgrounds, Gandhi being a devout Hindu and King a Baptist preacher in the South, both were deeply influenced by religious philosophy. Gandhi loved the Sermon on the Mount and would often quote from it in his speeches and prayer meetings. King, in his last speech delivered in Memphis, Tennessee, talked about the glory of God and reminded his audience that he had been to the mountain top.

During his college days, King studied and analyzed the techniques and methods Gandhi used to help win independence for India. He knew too well that America was not India and the culture of America was dominated by the glory of the gun. It was going to be difficult to adopt the Gandhi's methods because King was dealing with different people with a different political agenda. But he was sold on some aspects of Gandhi's methods, which, he thought, could be refined, adopted, and applied to solve social problems facing the black community.

What impressed King about Gandhi was his unwavering faith in the nonviolent method to tackle social problems. As a leader of Asians and blacks in South Africa, Gandhi used nonviolence to fight for their human rights. Gandhi understood well the meaning of discrimination from his first-hand experience and how the Indians in general but blacks in particular felt about discrimination. Even though he had a first-class railway ticket, he was thrown out on the platform on a cold night in South Africa.

Gandhi wanted to channel and direct the wrath of the oppressed community through nonviolent method. In his heart, he was thoroughly convinced that violence was counterproductive. He had tremendous success in South Africa in the application of nonviolent method and when he returned to India, he perfected his method to solve political and social problems. Like King, Gandhi met with opposition from many political parties and groups who scoffed at his methods. But

Gandhi stood firm in his faith and methods. He wanted India to win freedom through nonviolent methods only. He stated publicly that he would wait for hundred years to win India's freedom through nonviolent means rather than win it through violent way the next day. He never compromised on the question of nonviolence.

King was deeply impressed by Gandhi's commitment to nonviolence. Gandhi believed that good means alone could lead to good ends. In this he differed radically with communists and socialists in India, who believed that end justifies any means, including (sometimes requiring) violent means.

King was also opposed by many black groups who thought the white power structure could never be defeated by nonviolent means. They honestly believed that the white rulers should be given the taste of their own medicine of violence. Organizations like Black Panthers and to some extent leaders like Stokely Carmichael resorted to violence to achieve their political ends.

Like Gandhi, King did not compromise on the question of how to fight social discrimination. He knew he was on the right track and his method was going to be effective in the end. History proves that King was right and his opponents were wrong.

What impressed King the most about Gandhi's method was his advocacy and emphasis on civil disobedience to focus on social issues. Gandhi disobeyed the salt law peacefully and with prior warning in 1930. Thousands of men, women, and children participated in it and suffered British brutality peacefully. To Gandhi, salt was a symbol of a basic thing in life and the right of the people to make it. Through his technique of *satyagraha* (insistence on truth), he mobilized public opinion and challenged the mighty British empire.

As a student, King was aware of the thought contributions of Christ and Thoreau, who also used this technique (civil disobedience) to solve problems facing them. But theirs were individual experiments and never applied on a mass scale. King realized that Gandhi was the first leader in the world to use civil disobedience on a national scale. What worked in India under Gandhi's leadership, King convinced himself, could also work in America.

American culture is violent and the constitutional provision such as every citizen's right to bear arms had polluted the climate. It made King's task more difficult. But through his abiding faith in the nonviolent method and his skills as an orator, King successfully used the civil disobedience technique in challenging the Jim Crow laws in Alabama and Mississippi as well as throughout the United States. Through civil disobedience and the power of his voice, he mobilized public opinion against the injustices suffered by the poor blacks and whites alike. King convinced Southern politicians in Congress and his fellow preachers in the South to bring about long overdue social change to the South. His commitment paid off.

Another Gandhian technique that King used effectively was the technique of public boycott. Gandhi asked his followers to boycott English goods and schools and colleges that promoted English culture and preserved English interests. Millions of Indians burned English clothes publicly and started spinning and weaving (like Gandhi himself did) to make their own clothes and promote self-reliance. King used this method in Montgomery, Alabama, when Rosa Parks was not allowed to occupy the front seat in a public bus. The black community, inspired by Rosa's courageous example and under King's leadership, boycotted pubic buses to bend the white power structure and end the dirty bus practice of treating blacks as second-class citizens. It worked so effectively that the bus company could not afford to sustain such financial losses. Finally, it gave in. It was a great triumph for the black community. King's name became a household word. Unfortunately, neither King nor his followers, like Reverend Jesse Jackson, ever used the technique of public boycott on a national scale.

For example, funding practices of public black colleges and predominately white public colleges and universities in the United States is a blatant example of using public money to discriminate against black colleges who are struggling hard to meet the educational needs of minorities. This practice continues shamelessly, despite criticism from courts, chancellors of black colleges, and many educational reports. The black leadership has failed miserably to accept this challenge and to fight it through public boycotting and civil disobedience, if necessary, to redress the financial grievances of the black community.

As a follower of Gandhi, what has impressed me the most is the *moral courage* these two great servants of humankind showed in the face of opposition from the general public and from their own followers and friends. In the Indian National Congress annual meeting held in the holy city of Benaras in 1931, Gandhi openly criticized the wealthy Indian kings and princes, landlords, and the super-rich who were the members of Congress and dominated its leaders and controlled its programs. Gandhi told them to their faces that they never represented the poor Indian masses and that they needed to change their lifestyles to understand the toiling peasants. It enraged the rich community, and many Congress leaders asked him to shut up.

But Gandhi was one leader who would rather follow his faith than listen blindly to the leaders of the Indian Congress Party. Later, to maintain his independence, he even gave up his basic membership of the party. On matters of principle, he rarely compromised.

Now about King's example of rare moral courage. His test came during the heyday of civil rights movement (which coincided with the Vietnam War) in the 1960s. King knew well that a lot of black leaders like Whitney Young and Stokely Carmichael wanted him to confine his activities to civil rights only. They did not want him to dabble in political matters. In short, because he was a civil rights leader, they advised him to keep quiet on the Vietnam War issue. King refused to do this and risked his popularity and prestige and openly condemned the war as "immoral and unjust." He even criticized Congress and President Johnson for spending $1.5 million a day on producing war materials and spending no money for education and homes for the poor in America. King refused to be silenced. He followed his conscience. History tells us that King was right and the leaders who supported the war were dead wrong. Gandhi and King set up an excellent example for public leaders to follow when our leaders have to choose between their conscience and their constituents. Follow thy conscience in public life.

In the areas of means and ends, civil disobedience, pubic boycott, noncooperation, and moral courage, King followed Gandhi faithfully and with great success. But King didn't follow Gandhi entirely. For example, Gandhi's practice of undertaking a fast to influence the decision of his opponents and change their hearts never appealed to King for obvious reasons. Perhaps he felt that Americans would look upon it as a fad and never yield to such pressure. Cesar Chavez, another follower of Gandhi, used fasting to solve the problems of farm workers in California. But King was not convinced about the effectiveness of fasting as a method. He thought American culture and people were different and fasting wouldn't work here as such a tool..

Gandhi's life as explained in his autobiography, *My Experiments with Truth,* was full of experiments to reexamine his life in search of truth. He used a nature clinic to take care of his health, made homespun cloth to make his own clothes, and lived among the untouchables in New Delhi to focus the public attention on the plight of the poorest in India. He also experimented with new ways to vitalize India's educational system. In this sense, Gandhi touched every aspect of India to energize the country. It was a key to his great popularity and success as a leader. Gandhi's leadership was multifaceted.

King, on the contrary, was more or less a single goal–oriented leader. He neither experimented with different phases of life, as Gandhi did, nor did he live among the poor. King cared deeply about the poor. He fought for the rights of the garbage collectors and wept openly at the plight of the poor. Gandhi and King were both tremendously compassionate leaders. But King preferred to be a down-to-earth leader rather than experiment with Gandhian methods in America.

In short, Gandhi and King were two different but great leaders who served humankind according to their own inner light. They have certainly left behind their deep imprints on the canvas of humanity.

THE FOUNDING MOTHER OF THE
AMERICAN REVOLUTION

◗━━

I have read many books on the American Revolution and am impressed with the contributions made by our founding fathers, like George Washington, Thomas Jefferson, Benjamin Franklin, John Adams, and others. There is no question that these leaders risked their lives, some more like Washington and less like Jefferson and Franklin. But the dedication of the founding fathers and their commitment to the cause of liberty were unparalleled. Just think! If the American Revolution had failed, all the founding fathers and their close associates would most likely have been hanged. It was a treasonous act (against England), punishable with death.

Although I applaud these men for their great contribution in the achievement of freedom, I think a great injustice has been done to that great lady who helped her husband on the diplomatic front while taking care of her family during the most difficult times. It was a unique performance in those days especially considering that she was a woman! We have praised our founding fathers for their role in the American Revolution and have erected statues in the nation's capital. But we seem to have forgotten John Adams and his unforgettable wife, Abigail. If American people can forget John Adams, no wonder they have no memory of Abigail.

Has this happened because of oversight? No, it is the deep-rooted reflection of the American people who have hardly recognized the contributions of great women. They have always treated women as second-class citizens. Women didn't have the right to vote until 1920! When the U.S. Constitution proclaims that all men are created equal, they really meant "men" only. The signatories to the constitution paid a lip service to it because they talked about equality while Washington and Jefferson held slaves on their estates and Franklin kept quiet on the question of slavery for many years. But Adams was clear on slavery in principle and practice. He had no slaves on his farm, nor did he or Abigail supported slavery. Both of them were real revolutionaries in the real sense of the term.

In one of her letters, Abigail warned against dominating husbands. She had written, "I long to hear that you have declared an independency—and by the way in the new Code of Laws which I suppose it will be necessary for you to make I desire you would Remember the Ladies, and be more generous and favourable to them than your ancestors. Do not put such unlimited power into the hands of the Husbands. Remember all Men would be tyrants if they could." Abigail knew very well that under English law many wives were no better than indentured servants. They had no voice at home and no representation outside. She concludes by saying, "If particular care and attention is not paid to the Ladies we are determined to foment a Rebellion—and will not hold ourselves bound by any Laws in which we have no voice, or Representation."

What a woman! What a vision! Abigail was quite ahead of her times! By deeds, by actions, and by her contributions she was a revolutionary no less than Washington, Jefferson, and Franklin. Should we neglect Abigail because she was a woman?

It's time we had a statue of Abigail Adams in the nation's capital with her own words inscribed under it.

LEARNING FROM LIFE

⚬——

Life is a great teacher and teaches you many lessons if you are willing to learn.

What have I learned from life? First, nobody tells the whole truth in life or in the court. The reason is they do not *know* the whole truth. They do not have information to find out truth. More important, their decision is clouded by self-interest. If their friend or a relative is involved in a serious crime, they will not hesitate to lie in the court. They don't care as much for the truth as they do about their self-interest or the interest of their close friends or relatives.

Second, with all due respect for Mahatma Gandhi, I must admit that there is no such thing as one hundred percent non-violence. Even Gandhi had no answer to this fact. In 1942, when he served notice to the British government to leave India, some of his socialist followers asked for guidance to conduct the movement when all democratic doors were closed by the government. His reply to them is shocking: "Do or die." It means that do anything you want, including personal violence, to achieve Indian independence.

Martin Bauber, the Jewish philosopher, challenged Gandhi to apply his nonviolence method in Hitler's Germany. Gandhi's reply was far from convincing. His own followers wanted to solve the China-India border dispute through peaceful means. Some of them marched all the way to the shared border with China. But when the Chinese soldiers threatened to shoot them if they crossed the border, they retreated immediately. Gandhi's technique of nonviolence would not have worked in Hitler's Germany or Mao's China. It worked in India because as Joan Baez observed, the British were more "civilized."

Third, Buddha was perhaps the greatest secular leader that ever lived in this world. He was concerned more with compassion for humankind than with so-called religious rituals that characterized Hinduism during his time. He opposed and condemned them and fought them all his life. Buddha never believed in any gods or *moksha* (the heaven), as Hindus call it. His emphasis was on leading a good life. He came out with his golden rules for leading a good life.

Fourth, there is no guarantee in life. You may take exercise daily, gobble up all the vitamins from A to Z every morning, eat all the so-called healthy food twice a day, lead a stress-free life and never smoke, but still die before you are twenty-five! Two of my best friends—one a great wrestler and another strong in mind and body (he was a genius by any definition)—died before they were even twenty-eight! I am neither a wrestler nor genius, but I am enjoying a long and reasonably healthy life. How come? I have no explanation. Is it luck or grace of God? I don't know. This does not mean that one should not take exercise or stay away from your daily vitamins. Far from it. I exercise daily in the morning and take some vitamins to keep my heart healthy and get the energy. But it's no guarantee for prolonging my life. But I don't want to take a chance with my destiny. Who knows what's going to happen to me tomorrow?

Fifth, I have always believed in hard work in life. You can achieve many things in life through hard work. But success in life is a different story. Mere hard work at school or in a lab does not ensure success in life if you are not lucky. Luck plays a very important role in your life and ensuring success in your undertaking.

A friend of my mine is an outstanding chemist and is associated with a great company. He worked on a product for almost twenty-five years but did not get success, money, or recognition in his profession. But during the last seven or eight years, lady luck started smiling on him and one of his products proved to be an effective medicine for cancer. As a result, he shot into international fame, won many professional awards, and won very handsome cash awards. His life has changed now. He still works hard in his lab but with renewed energy. I have talked to some of his close friends who have been working on the same product, but they didn't succeed while my friend won prestige and many awards with lots of money. He was the only lucky scientist to have the breakthrough. What happened to the tireless efforts of others in the lab? They were just not as lucky as my friend.

Many work hard, but very few succeed in what they do. This does not mean that we should relax in our chair, drink coffee, and do nothing. It has also been found that lady luck sometimes smiles only on those who work hard.

I also believe that money is not related to academic education, experience, intelligence, or beauty. You have got to be lucky to be filthy rich. I can give two shining examples to prove my point. My sister in Bombay is not even a high school graduate but she was married to a businessman who made millions of rupees. They had no children. Unfortunately, her husband died of heart attack, leaving his millions to my sister, who has no investment experience. Here is another example. My daughter-in-law, who is not even a high school graduate, is married to my only son. My wife died leaving one and a half million rupees to both of them. They will probably inherit a good deal from me as well. I have a doctorate in education and have worked very hard and borrowed money from friends and universities to finish my schooling. In addition I was unsuccessful in two businesses. What happened to my experience and education? I am not lucky with money. But am I mad? No!

Finally, I'd like to comment on the way to be happy. Most people become miserable in their lives because they play the game of expectation and reward. Buddha had an answer for it. He showed all of us the road to eternal happiness. He told us that the root of all misery is the attachment to mundane things and our personal relationships with others. He instructed us to disassociate ourselves from worldly things. Once we do so, we win the lottery of happiness. In short, we become miserable because we expect something in return from everybody, including our friends and our relatives. When they fail to deliver the goods, we get mad or frustrated. Our expectations come with a price, or strings attached. *That* is the root of our misery and unhappiness.

Why don't we just do our duty and forget about expectations from others? How about trying unconditional love or an unconditional help to others? If our action is not reciprocated or rewarded, why should we worry about it? We have done our duty. How they react is not our concern. Leave the punishment or reward to the Lord. If you really want to be happy on this earth, don't take over His job!

A Plea for Parents

Teach us to love
The robins and rabbits in the wood
And not kill the helpless whales
For our ignoble livelihood.

Teach us to love
The truth and nothing but the truth
And sow the seeds of greatness
Before we embark on our youth.

Love us but don't use us
Like pawns in a chess game
For all of us will be losers
Without any victory or fame.

Since wars are first hatched
In the inscrutable human mind
Build in us the bulwark of peace
Before it's too late for mankind.